CREATIVE CONFLICT

How to Confront & Stay Friends

JOYCE HUGGETT

D1047723

INTERVARSITY PRESS
DOWNERS GROVE, ILLINOIS 60515

Published in the United States of America by InterVarsity Press, Downers Grove, Illinois,
with permission from Kingsway Publications Ltd., Eastbourne, England. Published in England under
the title Conflict: Friend or Foe?

InterVarsity Press is the book-publishing division of Inter-Varsity Christian Fellowship,
a student movement active on campus at hundreds of universities, colleges
and schools of nursing. For information about local and regional activities, write
IVCF, 233 Langdon St., Madison, WI 53703.

Distributed in Canada through InterVarsity Press, 860 Denison St., Unit 3, Markham, Ontario L3R
4H1, Canada.

Verses from Scripture are quoted from versions of the Holy Bible as indicated by the following:

NIV—from the New International Version. Copyright © *1973, 1978, International Bible Society. Used by*
permission of Zondervan Bible Publishers.

RSV—from the Revised Standard Version copyrighted 1946, 1952, © *1971, 1973 by the Division of*
Christian Education of the National Council of the Churches of Christ in the U.S.A., and used by
permission.

GNB—from the Good News Bible. Old Testament: Copyright © *American Bible Society 1976; New*
Testament: Copyright © *American Bible Society 1966, 1971, 1976.*

TLB—from The Living Bible. © *Tyndale House Publishers 1971.*

Cover photograph: David Singer

ISBN 0-87784-403-8

Printed in the United States of America

Library of Congress Cataloging in Publication Data

Huggett, Joyce, 1937-
   Creative conflict.

   1. Interpersonal relations—Religious aspects—
Christianity.   I. Title
BV4509.5.H83   1984   248.4   85-4733
ISBN 0-87784-403-8

16	15	14	13	12	11	10	9	8	7	6	5	4	3	2	1
97	96	95	94	93	92	91	90	89	88	87	86	85			

For David
with thanks for twenty-four years
of creative marriage

And with thanks to Joan
who typed the manuscript and gave
so much encouragement while the
book was being born

Preface

'How can two people who love each other end up hurting each other so badly?' The speaker was a friend of mine reflecting on the ruptured relationship with his wife. The tension that had built up between them over many years had finally erupted and they seemed powerless to hold their relationship together. In fact, their marriage illustrated the devastating effect of conflict.

Conflict, like molten lava pouring from a volcano, can burn up everything it falls upon, including potentially powerful relationships. The Christian church is littered with living testimonies of this sad fact.

I think of a service I once attended in a little church thousands of miles away from home. It was Easter Sunday. The scene seemed set for a joy-filled celebration. The sun forced shafts of gold through every open door and window. It poured its light on the white and green trumpets of the Easter lilies, played in the blonde hair of the Sunday-school children, and warmed the backs of the worshippers squeezing into the oak pews. There were people squatting everywhere: on chairs in the aisles, on the floor of the chancel, even on the altar rails. Some stood in the sun-drenched doorways.

With jubilant anticipation we sang the first hymn, 'Jesus

Christ is risen today. Alleluia!' We greeted one another, beamed at one another, and prayed together. In heralding the resurrected Jesus we were one.

'We will continue to celebrate the Lord's victory over death by singing some worship choruses. I'm sure you will see the relevance of the words.' The vicar's announcement was tinged with nervousness. I soon detected the reason.

'Choruses!' The very word seemed to send a shiver down the spine of many of the worshippers. They watched the lay reader reach for his guitar. Visibly, they froze. To express intimacy in song seemed foreign to their experience; perhaps beneath their dignity? Meanwhile others in the congregation responded gleefully. Accompanied by the guitar they praised God with joy, freedom and uninhibited devotion. But resurrection unity was broken. The congregation was split down the middle.

The next day I lay on the beach allowing the sun's rays to tan my body. I watched a mother play with her son. The small boy chuckled as she taught him to swim, giggled as together they hunted for 'sea creatures', laughed as his mother chased him in the wind. But a few minutes later he was sun-scorched and grizzly. His mother was cross and slapping him. Conflict spoiled their play.

My mind wandered back to England, to Geoff and Sally, a lovely young couple I met at a conference for newly-weds. They seemed very much in love: gazing into one another's eyes, holding hands. I liked them and admired their devotion to one another. But the day after the conference Sally arrived on my doorstep sobbing. 'Geoff's been violent again. This time he's hit me so hard he's bruised my arm.' Her presence reminded me of that pertinent question, 'How *can* two people who love each other end up hurting each other so cruelly?'

Conflict afflicts contemporary marriages, including Christian ones. It batters friendships, fellowships and families. It has a nasty habit of tearing people apart emotionally, leaving behind it a trail of destruction, loneliness and deep-seated hurt. It comes suddenly, unexpectedly, like a storm blowing in from the sea on a sunny day. Its force is frightening.

For this reason, like many others, I used to fear conflict and try to avoid it at all costs. It always seemed like a vicious onslaught from Satan. But over the years my views have been changing. I am beginning to see that conflict need not destroy. On the contrary, it is included in God's promise through Paul: 'We know that in all things God works for the good of those who love him' (Rom 8:28, NIV).

My husband and I, tracing the conflict that sometimes threatened to destroy our marriage, friendships or our church fellowship, are beginning to see that conflict is rather like the arrival of ET (Extra Terrestrial, for those who missed the film!) into one's world. On first acquaintance, ET seems a grotesque, repulsive, terrifying intruder, a foe to be expelled at all costs. His lovable qualities and his ability to transform self-centred lives emerge only gradually. Conflict is not unlike that. It peeps around the corner of marriages, committees, communities and church groups. It disrupts their comfortable self-centredness. It has the appearance of an unwelcome invader so we throw up our hands in alarm. Eventually it goes and those who have handled the situation well know that their lives have been changed for the better by God through the intervention of the seemingly detestable intruder who turned out to be a friend and not a foe.

'Those who have handled the situation well'. How *do* we handle conflict? Pretend it does not exist? Sweep it under the carpet hoping no one will notice? Run away from it as though it were an enemy? Exorcise it? Befriend it? Or what?

Where does conflict come from? Is it a subtle weapon wielded by Satan, the enemy of our souls? Is it a trust from God? Or does it originate in the open sores and sin-stained lives of weak-willed Christians?

These and allied questions are the themes that will occupy our minds as this book unfolds. It is my intention to show that Christians need never fear conflict. I aim to show that it need not be a dreaded foe. Rather, conflict can be a skilled teacher, a wise counsellor, a proficient, life-transforming friend.

My aim in writing this book is twofold. First, I hope to show *how* conflict can change lives for the better; how it can become as a sharp tool in the Master's hands, a tool that he uses, like a sculptor, to whittle away all that mars the beauty of the relationships he has entrusted to us. Second, I hope to shed light on conflict so that, when we stand like guilty bystanders, watching it destroy the lives of those we love with all the ferocity of a bomb-blast, we may not criticize: 'They're all Christians, why can't they forget their differences? It's a scandal.' But rather, uphold the situation, faithfully, prayerfully and compassionately, until the healing of reconciliation comes.

It is my prayer that through this book, some unnecessary conflict may be prevented, and that disintegrating relation-ships might be healed within the reconciling love of God; and that rather than dreading conflict, we Christians may dare to welcome it with cautious excitement and hope as we see it for what it is, the nerve-centre of growth, and learn to ask a fundamental question, 'Lord, how do you want to change *me* through this crisis?'

JOYCE HUGGETT

1
Conflict: Cause and Cure

One minute David and I were sauntering along in the warm sunshine, hand in hand, contented companions. The next minute pain prised us apart. One minute we were as one as we stood drinking in the grandeur of the scenery: blue sky, snow-crowned mountains, pink and white almond blossom, pillar-straight pines. The next minute it was as though a chill cloud blanketed this world. Yet there was not a cloud in sight. Only the silent hostility between us spoiled the splendour of the day.

It was hot. David, my husband, wilts in warm weather. We wandered into a supermarket.

'Look! Ice-cold drinks in the fridge! I'm going to buy some.'

'But they're all *fizzy* drinks. You know I don't like fizzy stuff. Let's go on a bit. There's a café on top of that hill out there. I can smell the coffee. We could sit in the sun, have a drink, and rest.'

'Coffee! Who wants coffee in this weather? Cold drinks are much better. Come on, let's buy some.'

I watched David choose a can of cool coke from the

fridge, swallowed my anger, and walked out of the supermarket in front of him. I was seething inwardly at this
demonstration of selfishness on his part. 'Couldn't he see
that I had needs too? Why, when we're abroad, does he
always insist on having all the money so that I couldn't even
go off and buy a cup of coffee on my own? Why doesn't he
listen when I state a preference?'

'D'you want a sip of my coke? It's very nice.'

David's teasing burst in on this silent stream of resentment. To his amazement I burst into tears, leaving him
wondering why my mood had swung so swiftly from
contentment to utter dejection.

'Is everything all right? Have I done something wrong?'

By this time the emotions rising inside me were so strong,
I dared not speak. I stood, silent, sullen, sorrowful, gazing
at the mountains and almond blossom whose still splendour
now seemed to mock me. Detached from David, I was
detached from this magnificence also. All I wanted was a
hole where I could take the ugliness of my emotions, empty
them out and hide until some sort of equilibrium could be
established between us again. But we were in Cyprus. I
knew of nowhere to hide. So we drove, in snow-cold silence,
back to our apartment, victims of conflict.

Conflict between Christians often erupts over trivia: the
choice of a drink on a hot summer's day, whether to decorate
the church for harvest with marrows or tins of baked beans,
whether to sing hymns or choruses during worship. Conflict
spreads stealthily, swiftly, unexpectedly. Like treading in
tar on the beach, or placing your hand on a live lizard while
picking wild flowers, conflict often comes as a nasty shock;
is often messy. And conflict wounds: both individuals and
intimate relationships.

What causes conflict? Is there a cure? How should Christians approach conflict: see it as an enemy, an intrusion, an
attack, or what? These questions launch us into our current
study of Christians in conflict with another question. How
can conflict become a transforming friend?

Causes of conflict: Satan

Conflict has created division among Christ's followers from Christianity's infancy until now. Think back to the last week of our Lord's earthly life. There we find the disciples quarrelling among themselves openly and in Jesus' presence (Mt 20:20ff., NIV). Or turn to Acts where you will read this of Paul and Barnabas, eminent church leaders: 'They had such a sharp disagreement that they parted company' (Acts 15:39). Peter, too, faced finger-pointing confrontation in Jerusalem, 'So when Peter went up to Jerusalem, the circumcised believers criticised him and said, "You went into the house of uncircumcised men and ate with them."' (Acts 11:2–3, NIV). Christians are still quarrelling among themselves. Many Christian leaders continue to indulge in cruel confrontation, and clergy-bashing is still one of the church's favourite pastimes. One reason for this is Satan's ceaseless and untiring activity.

It is now a well-established fact that for several years, Satanists in Britain have been fasting and praying for the break-up of Christian marriages. We need not be alarmed by this because in praying to Satan they are praying to the defeated foe. We need not be alarmed, but we must be aware and on our guard, ever watchful, ever prayerful. Satan and his minions are intimately interested in all wholesome Christian relationships. It was an unbeliever, a Cypriot agnostic, who opened my eyes to one reason for Satan's cunning.

Costas, not his real name, visits our church fellowship from time to time. On one occasion he admitted to me that he was inching his way towards the kingdom of God, moving from agnosticism towards Christianity. I wondered what had prompted his quest and this is what he said.

'I'm a person who *needs* friends. My wife and I have dozens of friends—we spend a lot of time with them. They matter to us. But when I visit your church, I see a quality of love I know nothing about. You Christians really know how to love one another—and I want what you've got.'

Costas' honest testimony beautifully illustrates Jesus' promise. 'By this all men will know that you are my disciples, if you have love for one another' (Jn 13:35, RSV). It underlines the fact that Christian relationships are potentially powerful. They attract people to Christ. They fill the love-gaps that yawn inside most of us.

Satan is not ignorant of these facts. He therefore takes an informed interest in all Christian relationships and schemes either to bring about their downfall or to pollute them. This is one of the reasons why conflict frequently flows, like a river of fire, through resourceful relationships that are deeply embedded in God. We find many examples of such Satan-induced conflict in the Bible.

Take Genesis 3, for example. Here we watch Satan sidle, •
snake-like, into the first marriage. He succeeds in looting the happiness of the first married couple. Moreover, with skill and cunning, he sets them against each other so that they accuse and blame one another. Where nothing but harmony once existed, strife now prevails. Satan has not changed his tactics. They are old, yet somehow ever-new. As one young married couple put it, 'For the past six months we've been caught in the cross-wind of Satan's most vicious attack.' Or, as a young Christian friend of mine once expressed it, 'Since getting engaged, I have felt Satan attacking me more fiercely than ever. I feel constantly up and down: guilty that I don't feel radiantly happy.' Or again, as a member of our own staff team put it: 'There are times when I can almost feel Satan trying to drive a wedge between us. He's on the rampage all the time.'

If you are engaged to a Christian or married to one, if you live in a Christian household or community or work in a Christian partnership or team, or even if your contact with Christians is minimal, expect tension. Expect conflict. Satan, the trouble-maker, the father of lies, has you on his visiting list. He visits to disrupt and to destroy. The Bible has provided us with clear procedural instructions for such eventualities. Fight (Eph 6:10) (Satan, not each other!). Resist (Jas 4:7). Be firm (1 Pet 5:8). Strive together (Phil 1:27). Pray (Eph 6:18). In other words, be on the alert and when the enemy strikes, take the initiative, with boldness, just as you do when silencing a barking but chained dog. When Christians take authority over Satan in the name of Jesus, Satan slinks away: a defeated, mangy lion.

Our responsibility, as Christians, is to hold two things in balance. We must take spiritual warfare and Satan's onslaughts seriously, not allowing ourselves to be beguiled into believing that Satan does not exist. He does exist. He is active. The Bible is clear on this. But we must not take an excessive or unhealthy interest in him. The Bible exhorts us to fix our eyes on Jesus, the author and finisher of our faith, not on Satan, faith's destroyer. And we must not be afraid of Satan. He is ever-active, but his power is limited; it is circumscribed by the victory Jesus won at Calvary.

The sin-stained self

Satan's power is limited, but it is not non-existent. On the contrary, it is subtle, persistent and irritating, because he knows where to strike to wound or to win.

One of Satan's subtle ploys today is to place the spotlight on himself; to encourage Christians in the belief that he is the source of *all* conflict. Thus when disagreements flare up or Christians begin hurting one another, we turn around, point the finger at Satan, and blame him. And Satan chuckles as he wins another round in the eternal battle—not because he had started the disagreement, but because those involved are now dodging their own responsibility. Most conflict originates, not with Satan, but a little nearer home. Most conflict finds its origin in our own hearts: in the sin-stained self. If we fail to acknowledge this, we absolve ourselves from taking full responsibility for the contribution we make to conflict. It is all too easy to say: 'It's not me. It's Satan.'

This happened to Geoff and Sally, whom I mentioned in the preface of this book. To recap, I met them at a conference for newly-weds where their apparent love for one another was a delight to watch. Subsequently they came to ask for help because Geoff's temper resulted in bouts of violence. He loathed himself for stooping to wife-beating and wanted to break free from the love-hate cycle he seemed to be treading. And Satan trapped him by sowing the seed-thought that he might be demon possessed.

'D'you think I'm demon possessed?' 'Don't you think I'm possessed with a spirit of anger?' he would ask from time to time. But there was no evidence of demon possession. There was a great deal of evidence of blatant, innate selfishness; the self-centredness that lashes out, even at loved ones, when it cannot have its own way. While Satan persuaded Geoff that a devilish agent was the cause of his violent outbursts, he demanded that *others* should do something about his problem: 'Deliver me from it'. But when eventually he saw that the true cause of the violence was himself, he knew that he had some hard work to do to co-operate with the Holy Spirit of God who is pledged to change us into the likeness of Christ.

The Bible leaves us in no doubt about the whereabouts of the root of much conflict. James puts it powerfully:

> Where do all the fights and quarrels among you come from? They come from your desires for pleasure, which are constantly fighting within you. You want things, but you cannot have them, so you are ready to kill; you strongly desire things, but you cannot get them, so you quarrel and fight (Jas 4:2, GNB).

Jesus, too, underlines that seeds of strife germinate in the inner recesses of man's heart: 'evil thoughts, sexual immorality, theft, murder, adultery, greed, malice, deceit, lewdness, envy, slander, arrogance and folly. All these evils come from inside' (Mk 7:20–23, NIV).

Paul has a neat label for this: 'the old nature'. In a moving paragraph in his letter to the Romans, he confesses that this old nature has not yet been fully transformed into Christ's image: 'I cannot understand my own behaviour. I fail to carry out the things I want to do, and I find myself doing the very things I hate... In fact this seems to be the rule, that every single time I want to do good it is something evil that comes to hand.... What a wretched man I am' (Rom 7:15–24, JB).

We twentieth-century Christians need the self-awareness and integrity of Paul to acknowledge that much of the failure in relationships resides in our own sin-pocked personality. We need the humility to come regularly to God and to plead, 'Lord, deliver me from the prison of my selfhood' (Thomas Merton's phrase). Our egocentric desires, our obsession with self and its appetites, the strength of the self-will—these are killers. It is why the 'I' must die. As we shall go on to discover, it is why conflict, with its capacity to oppose and to wound, is a friend in disguise.

The egocentric desires of others

Conflict is rather like a pack of cards. You have the king, Satan, and the ace, your own self-centredness. But there is also a joker: the self-centredness of others.

Just as I have been trained to live for number one, to feed her desires, so my husband, my teenage children and my brothers and sisters in Christ are equally egocentric, expressing their desires just as fiercely. The result, very often, is an inevitable clash of personality. As Christians we are learning to die to the sin-biased self that prevents us from becoming Christlike, but this dying is never instant, as we have seen. On the contrary, it is a long-drawn-out process. Meanwhile, we are like dying wasps, not only equipped to sting, but still capable of using that sting. When my brother or sister presses on an open sore in my life, leaving me frightened or in despair, or when someone seems wilfully to deprive me of something I felt I needed, I am not above wounding him. The dividing line between love and hate is wafer-thin.

The sinfulness of others poses some interesting problems. It sets up a series of reactions within me that aggravate and accentuate conflict.

First, the sinfulness of others makes me doubt my own ability to make wise choices. A friend of mine put this humorously on one occasion: 'I remember the third day of our honeymoon. It was a glorious, sunny, summer's day. I woke up eager to go walking, the only real way to explore the countryside. But my wife insisted that we go horse-riding. The strength with which she expressed her preference left me reeling. I panicked. What had happened to the sweet girl I'd married? Had I made some terrible mistake and married the wrong person?'

The self-centredness of others not only draws to the surface our own insecurity, it pinpoints our reluctance to forgive earth for not being heaven, to borrow Neville Ward's phrase. We expected our partner in marriage to be perfect—or at least to have attained a higher degree of perfection than we ourselves have reached. We surmised that our friend would sense our deepest needs and always meet them. We expected a *Christian* fellowship to be flaw-less. In other words, we place our Christian relationships on a pedestal that belongs, not on earth, but in heaven. And we must therefore continuously forgive our brothers and sisters for being as innately sinful, as weak-willed and rebellious, as we are ourselves.

This we are often reluctant to do. This reluctance to forgive earth for not being heaven and to forgive Christians for not being saints is matched by our inability to apply the grace of forgiveness to their specific weaknesses and failures. An imbalance creeps into our relationships. We expect others to forgive us, not just once, nor seven times, but to go the whole hog: to forgive us unceasingly, seventy times seven. Yet we dig our heels in, magnify our brother's faults, and refuse to cover him with the healing balm of forgiving love. The inevitable result of this withholding of love is redoubled selfishness. We think more highly of ourselves, our own growth, welfare and happiness than of the other person's, and thus we allow conflict to squeeze life from the relationship and from our brother also. But Jesus warned against such hard-heartedness. We are to forgive from the heart—'not seven times, but seventy-seven times' (Mt 18:21–22, NIV).

There is an escape route for such rebellious runaway feelings. Ranald Macaulay and Jerram Barrs put it helpfully:

> Notice that the commands to forgive and to forbear (as well as many others) assume the sinfulness of others. We should expect each other to be sinful, unpleasant at times, and difficult to live with. That is what it means to be a member of the human race at present. If we expect perfection from others or from ourselves, we will only succeed in being unable to appreciate anything that anyone does, or for that matter anything we do. To expect perfection from any but God is to crush them (*Christianity with a Human Face*, IVP, 1978, p.96).

Unmet needs

We must not only acknowledge that earth is earth, inevitable imperfection; we must also recognize that hidden factors add momentum to conflict in the same way as melting snow feed mountain streams in spring.

At the beginning of this chapter, for example, I recalled the quarrel that erupted between my husband and me, ostensibly over a thirst-quenching drink on a hot day in the mountains. When I stopped to analyse the events of that fateful start to a much-needed holiday, I realized that the question of the drink was simply the peg on which we were hanging the frustration of months.

We had been over-working; sacrificing our marital relationship on the altar of parish work: counselling, preaching, teaching, writing, befriending. We were well aware that overbusyness was siphoning off vital energy from our relationship: spiritual, sexual, emotional. We were depriving each other of time, attention and the cherishing on which zestful marriages thrive. Because of various crises in the parish, and because the end was in sight, we had been prepared for this to happen. 'We'll sort that out when we're on sabbatical' had become a cliché.

Now the much-longed for sabbatical was hours old. What was being expressed through the backbiting over a drink was the impatience we both felt as we waited for the resurgence of free-flowing love that comes with relaxation and deeply shared lives. What was also being expressed, albeit subconsciously, was the accumulation of months of unresolved tension and unmet needs. A month later, after we had unwound together, revised the art of relaxing together, studied and prayed together, that quarrel could not have flared up. By then we had rediscovered the joy of being sensitive to the other's needs; relearned the miracle-working power of gentleness, begun to thank God from the depths of our hearts for the mutuality of friendship we still give each other after twenty-three years of marriage.

Intimacy: the seed-bed of conflict

That is not to say that having rediscovered for ourselves the soul-satisfying joys of intimacy, no conflict could harass us again. No. Conflict is an integral part of all close friendships and of every good marriage. Intimacy breeds conflict. You can't have one without the other. In fact the closer two people become, the more they experience the oneness that was God's intention for married people, the more they open themselves to friction. This is inevitable. After all, they are attempting to fuse two imperfect, self-oriented persons: to so unite these two imperfects that they become one flesh.

It is important that we understand the correlation between conflict and intimacy because, as Christians, we are aiming to achieve an unprecedented degree of togetherness in our relationships. This is certainly true of the marital relationship. For years, married couples were content to create their marriage within a traditional framework. In traditional marriages, the role of both spouses was well defined, fixed. The husband's breadwinning role sent him outside of the home, while his wife's housekeeping, child-rearing role tied her to the house. If both partners fulfilled their roles with reasonable efficiency, the marriage earned the label 'successful'. If intimacy and companionship grew up between husband and wife, that was an uninvited bonus, a perk for which they were gratefully surprised. Such mutuality was not a prerequisite of a happy marriage.

Today, all that has changed. Couples marry not to fulfil a role, but for companionship: the giving and receiving of happiness and love. Their expectations of the marital relationship are high. Thus the door to conflict is swung wide open for, as Carl Jung once suggested, intimacy, the shared lives that make for marital union, constitutes an invasion of the individual ego which that personality naturally resists at first until it has developed an acceptable level of tolerance. Whenever a husband and wife set out to become more intimately involved in each other's lives, socially, sexually, spiritually, intellectually, emotionally, they automatically erect barriers that will prevent the other invading the privacy of their innermost being. Gradually, given time and sensitivity, a chink occurs in the fence. Eventually, in the healthiest, most intimate of unions, the fences are removed for at least part of the day. But this growth in intimacy takes time, patience, and a great deal of understanding love.

But it is not only marriages that are susceptible to the conflict that is an inevitable part of sharing one's life with another. Christian groups, too, with today's heavy emphasis on communication, sharing and support, are enjoying a oneness that has not been known in most churches for centuries. We are beginning to discover what the word 'fellowship' really means: compassionate, sensitive, appropriate love-in-action; the oneness for which Jesus prayed in his last recorded prayer on earth: 'I pray for them.... May they... be one... completely one' (Jn 17:9, 21, 22, 23, GNB); a reflection, however pale, of the interaction that always existed between the Father, the Son and the Holy Spirit.

This being so, church fellowships, with the coming together of differing—perhaps clashing—personalities, sometimes experience fierce and persistent conflict. This is hardly surprising when you think about it. Take our own church, for example. Church members are encouraged to join a house group, known as a Link Group, purely on the basis of geography. If you live in a certain area, you go to a particular group. I smiled as I drove home from one such group recently; marvelled that such a strange conglomeration of people could even begin to love one another. Some were old and set in their ways. Others were young and over-enthusiastic. Most had angularities that jostled rather than dovetailed with the angularities of the others. Between them they represented a startlingly wide range of tastes, values, theological persuasion and spiritual growth. In inviting them to form a cohesive whole, a certain amount of conflict is inevitable—even healthy. What impressed me was that the setting of such conflict was qualitative, mutual love; the desire to promote the welfare of others as well as the well-being of the entire group. Ten years ago, in our church, these people would not so much have nodded to each other at the church door. Now, we are encouraging them to explore what it means to be part of the body of Christ: members of the same family. That is why I say we have flung wide open the door to conflict.

Conflict: a life-changing friend?

Conflict is almost always painful, but when it is faced with the attitude that prevailed in this group, it becomes, not an invading enemy, but a life-changing friend. This friend provides the essential information individuals need to show them where they need to be changed by Christ. Conflict also specifies where the group as a whole needs to change so that each person matures, is nurtured and encouraged. Conflict strips groups and individuals of that besetting sin: selfishness. Conflict exposes specific sin.

The same is true of conflict in marriage and tension in the family. It was the quarrel over the cup of coffee I never had that spotlighted, for me, the resentments and frustrations I had stored up for months without even realizing it. Conflict not only triggered off this self-awareness, but resulted in the confession that leaves you feeling washed clean, as refreshed and new as a dust-covered palm tree douched by a heavy shower of rain. The conflict that pushed me into expressing the hurt I was feeling, enabled us to re-examine specific areas of insensitivity and neglect and to put them right. And this is the way of conflict. Ignore it and your relationships become like a war-torn city. See it as a trust from God and you will find your relationships are being constantly renewed.

I visited a war-divided city recently. One minute I was window-gazing in the colourful bazaar, the next minute a barbed-wire fence confined my movements and my every action was scrutinized by an armed soldier. I was on the threshold of enemy territory: a no-go area.

In many marriages, families and fellowships, there are no-go areas like this, subjects they dare not discuss: politics, nuclear disarmament, infant baptism, the fullness of the Holy Spirit. They cannot discuss them because an explosive situation would erupt. This is a pity because God uses conflict to hold up a mirror in which we may see ourselves reflected. This mirror does not distort, like the hall of mirrors at a fair. No. It reflects all too accurately the sin-infested me and makes a demand: 'This is how I want *you* to change.' That is why I make the claim that conflict need not be a foe; it can be a friend in disguise. Conflict is the friend who is ruthless enough to show me how God wants to strip me of my self-centredness, something that is often painful but necessary if I am to grow in the likeness of the Lord Jesus.

The cure of conflict

There is no cure for conflict this side of eternity. It is going to happen. No therapy, no palliatives, no preventive pills, no vaccination, are available to inoculate us against its invasion into the body. But then, as we have begun to discover, conflict is not a disease requiring a cure. On the contrary, conflict is to relationships what striving and struggling is to sticky horse-chestnut buds in spring: a burst of energy that, correctly channelled, results in prolific growth, the shedding of husks and eventual shelter for others. Our task in the remaining chapters of this book is to discover how, in the realm of relationships, such growth can be precipitated by conflict.

2
Friction in the Fellowship

Friction in the fellowship is inevitable. But friction in the fellowship need not be feared. Friction, the rubbing together of opposite, sometimes even opposing, viewpoints and personalities, is an integral part of firm relationships. Fellowship breeds friction. You can't have one without the other. In these days when the emphasis in the fellowship is on togetherness, sharing, being real, we must remind ourselves of this fact over and over again. Otherwise, individuals in the fellowship become as despairing as the magpie I found in my lounge one day last summer.

It was a balmy, breezeless day, so I flung open every window in the house. Some time later, strange noises greeted me from the lounge; a mysterious thumping and squawking. A magpie was flying at the window panes of the closed French window trying to escape. Freedom was only a pane of glass away, but he could find no way out. With each vain attempt to escape came a cruel collision: either of his black head against glass or his beak against the transparent barrier. After each abortive attempt, he would retreat, hurt and, I imagine, frightened and frustrated. He would sit under my desk squawking before trying again. Eventually, he gave up completely and curled up under my bureau, a silent, shivering, desolate figure. A few minutes later when I opened the French window, he refused to fly through it. Perhaps he was too shocked or too frightened to take the initiative by then?

Many members of Christian fellowships have tried, in vain, to forge wholesome friendships: to express love to one another as Jesus commands. In their attempt to create friendship they have been hurt by they know not what: they have become victims of conflict, that invisible something that inflicts untold pain. Some have recoiled, frightened, frustrated, numbed. Others have given up, unable to discover a way through. It is time to spread the good news that conflict is not the French window shut fast in our face. Rather, conflict can be the door flung wide, the way forward, the exit.

In this chapter, I propose to describe three real-life situations where Christians collided with one another in a conflict that left them as mystified as my magpie. I shall use these experiences to draw out strands that, if recognized, could help others to avoid such disharmony. I intend, too, to use these situations as a basis for an investigation of some questions that require an urgent reply. How does such conflict erupt? How do we conduct ourselves biblically when we are on such a collision course? How do we make conflict work for us?

Jeremy and Paul—pastor and assistant

Paul was a successful young executive when the Lord called him into full-time service. He and Anne, his wife, prayed long and hard before giving up their comfortable home and financial security to sacrifice it on the altar of the full-time ministry. But God seemed to have called and they knew they must therefore obey, whatever the cost to themselves or their children.

After two years of training, Paul and Anne emerged, full of missionary zeal, counting it a privilege to be involved in ministry together. They had visited the church where they were to work and were delighted to find that they related well to the pastor and his wife. They had also chatted amicably to certain key members of the congregation. Their expectations were therefore high. The pastor, his wife and their family would model to them what an ideal Christian family in leadership was intended to be, they would pray together as a foursome, and forge ahead as a team for the extension of God's kingdom. Of course, these expectations were never put into words. They assumed that Jeremy and his wife, like every other minister in the country, would share their ideals. They seemed so basic, so natural, so right to Paul and to Anne.

After they had settled down and the first-blush euphoria of early-ministry days had evaporated, Paul and Anne began to hear whispers about the pastor's teenage children. Words like rude, rebellious, standoffish were used to describe them. Then Jeremy's wife dropped the bombshell. For a variety of reasons—both financial and emotional— she had decided to take a full-time job. 'I really need to discover myself again after years of being buried under children, nappies and church work.' Not only was the novice's cherished, biblical family model proving to be a myth, but Jeremy's wife would not be alongside them in ministry, nor would she be available for supportive prayer and pastoring.

But Paul and Anne were resilient, optimistic, prayerful people. God had called them to work in this church. They were all Christians, so of course the relationship with Jeremy and his wife would eventually fall into place. Or so they hoped.

A year later, their dreams had crumbled and disillusionment had set in, like rain clouds on a November day. When I met them, they were all too ready to pour out their bewilderment and frustration.

Jeremy, who had seemed such a jovial character in the early days, turned out to be strong-willed; 'authoritarian rather than authoritative', Paul concluded. 'He's just like my father. If he's got an idea in his head, there it lodges and nothing I do or say can dislodge it. He never listens to me when I make suggestions. We never meet for prayer and rarely see them as a family. Apart from the working relationship between Jeremy and me, there's a non-relationship. It's so sad. There's so much potential in the area round the church and he's not tapping it, nor even attempting to meet the needs of the congregation. Anne and I do our best. We've got a lovely group of folk around us. They tell us how much they enjoy coming into our home, but they never darken the doors of Jeremy's house. They tell us they wouldn't take their problems to Jeremy or his wife. They just wouldn't understand. And anyway, his wife's now so busy doing her own thing, she really hasn't got time for anything or anybody.'

After a year of working as colleagues, Jeremy and Paul were locked in conflict; a conflict that was percolating through the church, reaching the people sitting in the hard pews every Sunday, and threatening to split the church in two: the pro-Jeremy's and the pro-Paul's. And I imagine Satan watched them attempt to lead their people in the worship of God, rubbed his hands with glee and chuckled.

Rob and Mark

At least Jeremy and Paul were still talking to each other. When Rob and Mark each came to see me, they had ceased to do even that.

Rob is a strong-willed, talented young man in whom God has invested clear leadership gifts. He is hot-headed, but sensitive too. In the past he has been emotionally wounded by his inflexible, irresponsible father. Mark is an older man, full of zeal for God, single-minded in his aim to bring unbelievers into the kingdom of God. His aim in life, like the psalmist's, is to obey the word of God implicitly, not to veer from it in any way. When other Christians fail to live up to his high standards, an intolerant streak within causes him to question whether they really have been born again.

Rob and Mark were invited to co-lead a group. Rob was excited. Mark and his wife were older than he; he and his wife would be able to learn from their maturity. Mark would be the reliable father he had never had. He looked forward to being pastored by him. He would grow and thus his usefulness for the Lord would increase. Mark, too, approached the joint leadership prayerfully and with enthusiasm. He admired Rob's love for the Lord; looked forward to delegating certain responsibilities to him. He trusted Rob, a man he considered to be 100% for Christ.

But Rob and his wife, unknown to Mark, were struggling with marital difficulties brought on by cramped living conditions (they and their children lived in one room of a friend's house), financial pressures and the disorientation that plagues some people when they move from place to place. (Rob and his family had recently moved and were making the necessary readjustments very slowly.) These underlying tensions triggered off frequent quarrels. It was not unknown for Rob to hit out at his wife in frustration and anger.

One day, in despair, Rob sought Mark's advice about the marital disharmony that was causing him so much distress. It was as though someone had pricked a balloon. 'Rob? Guilty of wife-battering? How could he be a Christian then?' Questions like these tormented Mark and prevented him from hearing Rob's anguish and desire to discover a way forward. Mark's mind was fixed on the fast-vanishing, idealized and unreal image that he had projected on to Rob. Rob now stood before him, no longer one of God's giants, but, in Mark's eyes, a despicable failure. Such 'failure' lay outside his ability to understand either the grace of God or the complexities of human relationships.

Rob sensed Marks' disapproval of him and recoiled, baffled, dismayed. In the past, when problems of a similar nature had flared up at home, he had sought counsel from an older Christian and been helped. It had never occurred to him that Mark would be thrown off balance by his personal problems. 'If I can't go to Mark for counselling, to whom can I turn?'

Into their once-harmonious relationship, bitterness, resentment and suspicion came crowding in. At first, they retreated from each other. Then they tried to forgive each other. But the hurt each had inflicted on the other was never discussed. It was buried, live, to fester and to cause trouble on a subsequent occasion.

That occasion came a year later when Mark's vision for the group clashed with Rob's. Rob challenged Mark's leadership. Mark retaliated by attacking Rob. They talked and they prayed and they quarrelled. Members of the group grew increasingly aware of their disintegrating relationship. Fractions were formed—the pro-Rob's and the pro-Mark's. Unhelpful gossip split the fellowship further. By the time Rob and Mark discussed the situation with me, there seemed to be only one solution—a Paul and Barnabas-style separation.

A group in conflict

Or, I can think of a group of Christians where relationships had soured through conflict. This group had been left leaderless unexpectedly. One of the members, with the encouragement of the staff of the church and the group, assumed leadership. At first the group rallied round her, supported her, recognized that hers was a difficult role. But then, criticism after criticism was levelled at her. She spent less time with them than the previous leader had done. Her leadership style was brought under question. Even her spirituality was scorned.

Leaders have feelings. Criticism, like fire-tipped darts, pierced this girl's sensitive spirit, wounding her deeply. She threatened to abdicate leadership. It was at this point that I encountered the group and together we tried to unscramble some complex and now-poisoned relationships.

We must now hold those incidents in our mind. Place alongside them similar incidents known to you. Recognize that certain themes repeat themselves, like the recurring theme in a piece of music. Our first task is to recognize what these themes are, to give them names and to seek to understand a little more about them.

Unrealistic and unclarified expectations

The first common denominator is this: unrealistic and unclarified expectations. In each situation, conflict arose because the Christians concerned cherished unrealistic expectations of the relationships or the people involved. Take Paul and Anne's expectations for example: Jeremy and his family would model the perfect biblical family to them. They would pray together regularly, enjoy friendship and a vital team ministry. None of these expectations are wrong in themselves, but Paul and Anne could have saved themselves a great deal of heartache if they had clarified beforehand whether Jeremy and his wife shared these expectations and whether they had the necessary resources to meet them.

Or take Rob and Mark. Rob assumed that Mark would want to be a father substitute, and that God had invested counselling gifts in him. Mark assumed that Rob was transparent. Expectations were never discussed, only dreamed about. Had they been shared it would have become apparent early on that they were unrealistic.

The same ingredient was active in the group. I asked them to be totally honest, to spell out their expectations of their leader. As they did so, we all began to laugh. Not a single person known to any of us could have hoped to match even half of those expectations.

Unclarified expectations in fellowships, as in marriage, frequently result in disillusionment, frustration and despair, because when we nurse unrealistic hopes of another person or relationship, there is only one thing that person or relationship can do. Fail. Such disillusionment is to promising relationships what rust was to my old car. A killer. Disillusionment generates bitterness, resentment, jealousy and hostility. These eat into even the sweetest of relationships unless the persons creating the relationship are working towards the same goal, sharing the same vision and living accordingly.

Lack of affirmation and appreciation

Another thread that weaves its way through the three situations I have described is the critical spirit that fails to affirm others and fails to appreciate them. Paul and Anne, for example, showed a complete absence of affirmation or appreciation of Jeremy, his wife or their ministry. Indeed, it was with some venom that Paul made the comment, 'He's not tapping the potential of the area', and I sensed a shade of sick glee when he observed that nobody would take their problems to Jeremy or his wife. 'Was Jeremy all bad?' I wondered. 'Did this ministry, family life and personality warrant such a totally negative response?'

Lack of affirmation and appreciation also characterized Mark's attitude to Rob and Rob's attitude to Mark. It was as though Mark could no longer see the zeal he once so admired in Rob and that was still there; as though Rob was now blind and deaf to Mark's devoutness although that had not changed. And the group I mentioned were so over-flowing with criticism for their leader that none of them had stopped to thank her for the things she *was* doing well. They concentrated on condemning her for her failure.

This destructive habit of zeroing-in on the failures of others, even magnifying them, is all too common. It causes negative emotions to throb through our entire being like a drum-beat that cannot be stopped. Like finding a dead sheep in a stream, it crowds out much of the beauty in the world around us. It even blinds us to the Lord's goodness. And it renders us insensible to the worth of the person(s) we are growing to hate.

C. S. Lewis, in *The Screwtape Letters*, shows that this is Satan's work and that his methods are cunning:

> When two humans have lived together for many years it usually happens that each has tones of voice and expressions of face which are almost unendurably irritating to the other. Work on that. Bring fully into the consciousness of your patient that particular lift of his mother's eyebrows which he learned to dislike in the nursery, and let him think how much he dislikes it. Let him assume that she knows how annoying it is and does it to annoy.... And, of course, never let him suspect that he has tones and looks which similarly annoy her.
>
> As he cannot see or hear himself, this is easily managed (*The Screwtape Letters*, Fontana edn, 1960, p.22).

Satan is out to prise Christians apart, to ensure that any cleavage between them widens, that reconciliation is improbable. When we fail to affirm people, that is, when we fail to upbuild their strength through our appreciation, we aid and abet Satan and thwart the purposes of the God who is quick to affirm, swift to applaud. 'I have not found faith like this in Israel.'

The second time I met with the group I described, I reflected my observations: a series of soured relationships. I invited them to go away, make a list of every member of the group, and to write against each name the qualities they respected or admired in that person, then to bring their findings to our next meeting. 'Now tell the people concerned what you have written on your piece of paper,' I said.

I shall not easily forget the looks on some of the faces in the room that night as those whose relationships had been characterized only by hatred in recent months, heard themselves affirming the much-loathed brother or sister in Christ. It was as though we watched Satan fall before our eyes. Defeated.

Lack of understanding

Friction in the fellowship is frequently caused because we do not know and understand one another as whole persons: the person who comes to church also goes to work, relaxes, lives in a home. It very often happens that when we seek to understand our opponent, conflict slides away like snow dropping off the roof tops when the sun shines. It is as Paul Tournier observed: 'One who feels understood feels loved.'

To understand another is the prerequisite of true love. To love another means to understand him. A lack of understanding of the needs and predicaments of others runs through the stories I have mentioned like a ladder in a stocking.

Paul and Anne, for example, had failed to take into consideration that Jeremy's wife was suffering from menopausal depression and that the inevitable repercussions in the household were disruptive. Similarly, the group seemed incapable of putting themselves in their leader's shoes, or acknowledging that hers had been the unenviable task of taking over the leadership without preparation or due warning; that she was still eclipsed by her much-respected predecessor. And Mark seemed not to have heard that well-versed saying, 'Don't criticize your brother 'till you've walked a mile in his moccasins.' He seemed not to have asked himself how he might have coped with the pressures troubling Rob: sharing a bedroom with his children, living on a shoestring budget, meeting constant work deadlines.

Blaming, attacking, accusing

Paul says in his epic ode to love, 'love is patient, love is kind. It does not envy, it does not boast...it keeps no record of wrongs. Love does not delight in evil but rejoices with the truth' (1 Cor 13:4–7, NIV). But the people I have mentioned *did* store up wrongs, *did* rejoice in evil, *were* unkind. The devilish threesome—attacking, blaming and accusing—crept into their mentality and vocabulary. The Paul in my example attacked, not just Jeremy's inefficiency, but Jeremy's person also. Members of the group used phrases like, 'The trouble with you is...', 'You always...', 'You never...', when they complained of their leader.

Such vocabulary is Satan-designed to create conflict and to crush people. Instead of falling prey to such sarcasm and backbiting, we must learn to ask of God a profound question. 'Lord, what is it about *me* that needs to change? What is it about *me* that is unable to cope with this relationship?' This shifts the focus in a healthy way from our opponent on to ourselves. It is one of the ways to work at conflict as an assignment. God is relentless in showing the answer to such questions. They are the key to using conflict creatively.

Creative conflict: communication

Conflict erupts, as we have seen, with all the heartbreak of a forest fire. How can Christians make conflict work for them? How do we live biblically at such times?

If conflict between Christians is to become constructive, not destructive, we must learn to communicate remembering Paul's admonition to speak the truth *in love* (Eph 4:15). Jesus emphasizes the importance of clear communication in the face of conflict:

> If your brother sins against you, go and show him his fault, just between the two of you. If he listens to you, you have won your brother over (Mt 18:15, NIV).

> Therefore, if you are offering your gift at the altar and there remember that your brother has something against you, leave your gift there in front of the altar. First go and be reconciled to your brother; then come and offer your gift (Mt 5:23, NIV).

The first thing we must do if conflict arises is to obey Jesus. If you are at variance with a fellow Christian, go and talk to the person concerned. What often happens in Christian circles is the exact opposite. Take Paul, the assistance pastor, for example. He was hurt by the disintegrating relationship with Jeremy, the pastor. Instead of talking this through with Jeremy, he poured out the hurt to people in the church. This proved divisive. People were forced to play piggy-in-the-middle between the two pastors. This is unbiblical. Jesus said, if your brother has hurt you, go and talk to *that* brother.

But, of course, the way we talk to the brother is crucial. The encounter must be steeped in love and it must take full responsibility for the brother's feelings. Therefore, blaming and accusing and condemning are inappropriate. Instead, some words of Paul must rule our conversation:

> Be completely humble and gentle; be patient, bearing with one another in love. Make every effort to keep the unity of the Spirit through the bond of peace (Eph 4:2–3, NIV).

> Get rid of all bitterness, rage and anger, brawling and slander, along with every form of malice. Be kind and compassionate to one another, forgiving each other, just as in Christ God forgave you (Eph 4:31–32, NIV).

Good communication is not something that just happens to us like catching measles. Good communication has to be learned. Good communication is the ability to convey messages, emotions and attitudes to another person as accurately and as lovingly as possible. It also includes the ability to receive such messages from another person without filtering those messages through the wire-mesh of our preconceived ideas. It means, among other things, checking out meanings rather than assuming that you have understood correctly. 'Do you mean...?' 'Are you saying...?' This dimension of communications is vital. When relationships between two people break down you will often hear each one say, 'I thought you felt...' 'I thought you said...' You can avoid this kind of misunderstanding by clarifying 'Am I correct in thinking...?'

And we must spell out the situation as we see it. Say it

straight. '*I feel* angry because you forgot to tell me that the sermon was to be fifteen minutes instead of half an hour.' '*I feel* hurt because you failed to understand my anguish the other night.' 'I feel...' is a much more loving and accurate prefix than 'You don't...', 'You didn't...', 'You never...', 'You failed...'. Not: '*You didn't* tell me that my sermon was to be fifteen minutes instead of half an hour.' '*You failed* completely when it came to understanding me the other night.'

This is not nit-picking; playing with words. If my colleague admits, 'I feel unsupported by you...' we can explore together whether his feelings are the best gauge of the situation or not. It could be that the facts and his feelings contradict one another. And by saying it straight, my colleague gives me the opportunity to identify with his hidden hurts. But if he comes to me and blurts out, 'You don't understand me', my reaction might be negative. In the face of such an attack most of us become defensive, even aggressive.

But if we are to encourage other people to 'say it straight', 'this is how it feels...', then we have to become skilled in receiving those feelings. There must be a willingness within the fellowship to listen to others, and to listen at depth. By this, I mean we must be willing to learn to weigh the other's point of view, sensitively and compassionately and, where we have failed, to apologize. In order to do this effectively we must learn to tune into the multi-level exchanges offered when a person is trying hard to communicate. This means listening to the tone of voice, the facial expression, body movements, hand gestures, as well as the words used. We can learn a lot about the person through his eyes: perhaps they are hollow and sorrowful, tear-filled, or flashing with anger. And we must bear in mind that the most effective communication takes place when touch, tone, face, body and words communicate a single message; that when there is a disparity the non-verbal communication usually reflects the real situation most accurately. So if a person *says* 'I'm fine' but their face is pale and their eyes are sad, believe the messages of the eyes rather than that offered by the lips.

Good communication is vital. Without it, relationships fragment, resources are dissipated, and hurts are not healed. When Christians communicate at cost to themselves, communicate in depth, and communicate with others in the reconciling atmosphere of prayer, conflicts are quickly resolved.

Commitment

The Chinese symbol for crisis is made up of two characters. One means 'danger', the other means 'opportunity'. Christians who are committed to one another are those who are committed to treat conflict as homework to be done, who resolve to benefit from it and learn from it. They are wise enough, in the face of conflict, to ask certain questions: 'Are we *for* each other or against each other?' 'Do we want this relationship to work to glorify Christ, or is the price we may have to pay too high?' 'Lord, is there something in *me* that is disrupting this relationship?'

These are the questions we must ask when we are locked in conflict with another as Mark was with Rob, as Paul was with Jeremy. Isn't this what the apostle Paul meant when he exhorted the Philippians to 'strive together' or when he admonished the Ephesians to 'make every effort to keep the unity of the Spirit'? The picture is of Christians straining every nerve and muscle, pulling together like the members of a boat crew, striving to reach the goal: unity. Anything that falls short of this commitment is to be confessed and I am not allowed to pin the blame for crab-catching on my brother.

Of course, this kind of commitment is costly. It is the commitment without which conflict may lead to the demolition of relationships: marriages, partnerships, friendships, families. This kind of commitment, 'We're in it together, by the grace of God we *will* make it work', is an essential foundation for all Christian relationships, particularly for fellowship groups.

Such groups, like their secular counterparts, move through three distinct phases. First, there is the honeymoon period when everyone is enthusiastic, determined to pull together with the others. This phase is often characterized by excessive dependency on the leader who, at this stage, in the eyes of the group, cannot put a foot wrong. They commit themselves to one another with eagerness. But the dynamics change. The groups grows up. It travels through an adolescent phase. Like adolescents, individuals challenge, question and rebel. The leader no longer sits secure on her pedestal. Her leadership may be under close, even critical, scrutiny. If the group and the leader are committed to making the relationships work, they weather the storms of this second phase and learn from them. They then sail into the third, and calmer, phase where the group and leader level with each other, see themselves as equals, and relate in a healthy adult—adult fashion. Without commitment, the group may collapse at any stage like a house made with dominoes and never enjoy the benefit of phase three.

Confession

Whenever a crisis erupts the human reaction is to find someone to blame. 'It's that toad, Satan, again.' 'It's the pastor.' 'It's the elders.' 'It's the organist.'

Jesus speaks right into this normal, understandable series of reactions with this challenge:

> Why do you look at the speck of sawdust in your brother's eye and pay no attention to the plank in your own eye? How can you say to your brother, 'Let me take the speck out of your eye,' when all the time there is a plank in your own eye? You hypocrite, first take the plank out of your own eye, and then you will see clearly to remove the speck from your brother's eye (Mt 7:3–5, NIV).

If we are to live biblically, the critical spirit, boasting, subtle emotional swiping of another, inappropriate jealousy, rivalry, slander, must all go. They must be replaced by the humility of spirit that takes conflict seriously, desires reconciliation, and therefore asks 'Lord, show me where *I* have failed. Bring me to the place of repentance.'

God will answer this prayer if we make it with integrity. The self-examination involved should result in confession to God and maybe to the people we have wronged also. And, of course, as we enjoy the forgiveness God delights to give to his penitent children, we must in turn freely forgive our brothers and sisters in Christ.

To say sorry and to forgive is not easy. But there are essential disciplines for those who would learn the creative use of conflict. If we refuse to forgive, we shall be taken over by resentment, bitterness and fear. This indwelling hostility generates the energy for wrecking relationships further. Like Jesus we must forgive, not just those we are fond of, but our persecutors also. Like Jesus we must hold into the reconciling love of God the unholy tangle that surrounds conflict. Like Jesus, we must trust that the whole of life is in God's hands so that we learn to bear the brunt of conflict without retaliation.

Clarification

As we struggle to communicate and strive to commit ourselves to others, as we seek to keep short accounts with God through confession, so we must also clarify in our minds what Christian relationships are all about. Take Jesus as the model, and one word emerges: servanthood.

Think back to Paul and Jeremy, pastor and assistant, and the expectations Paul brought to that relationship. If, instead of asking, 'What can the pastor and his family *give* me?', Paul had asked a different question, 'How can I *serve* them?', the relationship would have taken an unexpected, but wholesome, turn. Similarly, if the group had asked, 'How can we serve our leader?' the group dynamics would have done a welcome somersault.

And this is what we are required to do if we are followers of Jesus. We should cease to be obsessed with the 'What's in it for me?' mentality. Instead, the humility of Jesus should be our focal point: 'Whoever wants to become great among you must be your servant, and whoever wants to be first must be slave of all. For even the Son of Man did not come to be served, but to serve, and to give his life a ransom for many' (Mk 10:43, 44, NIV).

In other words, the Holy Spirit turns worldly expectations on their head so that, in diagrammatic terms, the relationship between Paul and Jeremy looks like this:

A		B	
God		**God**	
Pastor		**Assistant pastor**	
Assistant pastor		**Pastor**	

Human expectations	**Christian leadership**
The pastor, in submission to God, assumes responsibility for the assistant pastor who serves both	The assistant pastor, in submission to God, assumes responsibility for the pastor who serves both

And the group looks like this:

A		B	
God		**God**	
The leader		**The group**	
The group		**The leader**	

Worldly expectations	**A Christian pecking order**

In worldly terms the leader is more important than the group. In Christ, the roles are often reversed. The true situation is not either **A**, or **B**, but both **A** and **B**. This is the meaning of mutuality: shared servanthood.

If we are to live biblically when friction threatens the fellowship, it might help to draw a diagram like the one above, to write the names of the people concerned in their pecking order, then to turn the diagram upside down. We must remind ourselves of this concept of servanthood frequently, the mutuality that Paul discusses in Ephesians 5:21: (GNB): 'Submit yourselves to one another because of your reverence for Christ'.

It will also be important to ask oneself a series of questions: 'What am I expecting from this relationship, this person, this situation?' It sometimes helps to clarify your thoughts if you write down your hopes and expectations. Examine them. Place them alongside the real group of people involved. Ask: 'Are my expectations reasonable: realistic? Am I, perhaps, setting up a situation in which others can only fail? Lord, how do you want my expectations to be pruned, revised, and brought into line with your will?'

Your own hopes and expectations are only one side of the coin. The other people involved cherish expectations too. These must be placed alongside your own so that the two dovetail, but this dovetailing might necessitate some radical changes. You may need to change. Others may need to change also. We must never scheme to bring about changes in others. Our responsibility is to allow the transforming Spirit of God to change *me*; to hold the entire situation before God in prayer.

In order to establish what some of the required changes are, fellowships and friends, families and marriage partners should stop from time to time to examine: What am I hoping for from this relationship or group? What can I give to it? If all the parties concerned place their hopes alongside one another and if all are committed to one another and to living biblically, deadlock will be minimal and exciting growth will be a very real possibility as the following equations suggest:

non-communication + lack of clarification = confusion = conflict

conflict + communication + clarification + commitment = growth

Making conflict work for you

If friction is to result in fruit-filled lives, we must allow it to be our teacher, the one who shows me where *I* need to grow in wholeness and maturity. We must allow it to be our communication-facilitator, the one who persuades *me* to learn the invaluable art of transmitting and receiving accurate messages. We must allow it to be our guide, the one who helps *me* to explore the mystery and cost of commitment. We must allow it to be our pastor, the one who supports but challenges and brings everything under the reconciling hand of God. And we must allow it to be an umpire, one who sees that each person concerned stoops to servanthood without being reduced to a doormat. Certain questions help us in this quest for creative conflict. I repeat them here because they are irreplaceable stepping stones to conflict resolution:

1. What am I expecting from this fellowship/relationship?
2. What can I give to it?
3. Are my expectations realistic?
4. What do I appreciate about the person with whom I am locked in conflict?
5. What is it about me that refuses to acknowledge the good in him/her?
6. What is it about me that finds it hard to voice his worth?
7. What is it about me that does not want to support him?
8. What is it about me that needs to change?
9. What is it about me that cannot cope with this relationship?
10. Are we *for* each other or against each other?
11. Do we want this relationship to glorify God?
12. Is there something in me that is disrupting the unity of God's people?

13. Lord, show me where I have failed. Bring me to the place of repentance.

Examine your replies to these questions with care. Confess any disobedience to God. Repent. (Repentance means determining to live differently, turning your back on sin.) Go back to your fellowship pregnant with God's love for each person and watch a miracle unfold.

3

Friction between Friends

Last summer I fell off a ladder. The damage amounted to nothing more than a poker-stiff arm and a cluster of saucer-sized bruises. Even so, as I mused on my clumsiness, I became acutely aware of feverish activity taking place in my body. Blood was racing to the wounded parts; it burned with comforting heat as it carried a consoling message, 'Healing is coming—fast.' I offered silent thanks for the chemical reactions that the body sets in motion whenever an injury takes place, the discomfort that precedes healing.

Two months later, the work-load I was trying to carry weighed on me like a heavy burden. I expressed this to my colleagues. Their sensitive handling of the situation and of my battered emotions communicated a similar message of comfort. 'We're on your side. We care about you. We want to help.' I thanked God for people and reflected that friendship is one of the most precious gifts God gives. Just as the body pulsates to heal, so the love of friends sustains, holds and restores. It is as Margaret Evening observes, 'Life without true friendship is hardly life at all' (*Who Walk Alone,* Hodder & Stoughton, 1974, p.38).

In the next two chapters, I propose to place the spotlight on this precious gift, friendship, and to examine certain questions. Why is friendship vital to our sense of well-being? Why are friendships, even among Christians, frequently disrupted? How do we go about repairing the ruptures?

Friendship: a fundamental necessity

Friendship is not an optional extra for the fortunate few who strike up friendships easily. Friendship for human beings is a fundamental necessity. The reason for this is that God made man in his own image, needing to give and receive love. The doctrine of the Trinity reminds us how important a part a loving relationship has to play in the very nature of God. Mankind was born for relationship. Denied of this opportunity, man, even before the Fall, plumbed the depths of loneliness. God sensed this loneliness and observed that it was 'not good'. It prompted him to create human relationships. The perfect mutuality enjoyed by Adam and Eve before the Fall can never be our post-Fall experience. Nevertheless, friendship continues to be vital for our health and our growth. The earthly life of Jesus demonstrates this. Jesus, the perfect, whole man, needed friends. Jesus valued friendship. (For a fuller discussion of this subject, see my book, *Growing in Freedom*, IVP, 1984.)

If friendship is so strengthening, even healing, why do Christian friendships suffer the disruption that frequently tears friends apart? We eavesdrop on Marian and Joy's disintegrating relationship in our search for one answer to this perplexing problem.

Marian and Joy

Marian and Joy were firm friends. Marian was married; Joy was single. They both led busy lives but had many things in common: walking, a love of nature, a love of solitude, music. And Joy loved to spend an evening in Marian's house.

Whenever they were together their minds seemed to meet. Marian appreciated this. After years of bringing up children, it felt so good to talk to someone like Joy who was steeped in the world of ideas.

Marian could never put her finger on one reason why the relationship began to deteriorate. 'As far as I can recall, it all goes back to one phone call,' she told me. 'Joy seemed so different. I'd upset her for some reason and the way she spoke to me just creased me. When I put the phone down, I burst into tears. After that, I wept for days and days. Then my husband got angry. "The friendship's not worth it," he said. "Forget it". But the friendship really matters to me. I don't want to forget it. And anyway, I want to find out the reason for this childish behaviour of mine. Right at this moment, Joy has withdrawn from me and I find myself hating her for that. But I know that, as a Christian, I shouldn't store up bitterness. I want to be rid of all these negative feelings.'

Shadows of the past

'Marian, does Joy remind you of anyone in your past? Mother maybe? Or father? Are her looks, mannerisms, tone of voice, reminiscent of an authority figure?'

'It's funny you should say that. I've sometimes thought after Joy's gone, that it's been just like talking to my mother—just the way it was when I was a little girl.'

Marian surprised herself by pouring out the deep-seated hatred for her mother that she had carried around with her, unacknowledged, since she was quite young, the same sort of unmanageable bitterness she now felt towards Joy. This proved to be the tap-root of her rotting relationship with Joy.

Stored wraths of the past

We need to understand what is happening here because this process is not uncommon. Indeed, it is a frequent cause of friction between friends. You seek to relate closely with a particular person in the present. Without anyone realizing how or why, that person or situation reminds you, albeit subconsciously, of someone in your past whom you feared, or resented or to whom you felt hostile for some reason. You stored away these wraths, maybe in childhood, maybe in adolescence, or maybe earlier in adulthood. You buried them inside you, deep down where neither you nor anyone else would see them. But they were not buried dead. No. They were buried live, like active ingredients in nuclear waste. These dormant emotions lie in wait until a situation occurs in the present that is not unlike the past. They then set to work again with all their destructive power. This is what was happening to Marian. The bitterness and hatred and insecurity that she buried because of the impoverished daughter-mother relationship became active again affecting her relationship with Joy. Marian not only felt the strain; her perspective became blurred. At times it was not Joy she was relating to at all, but her mother.

When the submerged hostilities of the past surface and force us to pay attention to them again, one of two things may happen. Like Marian, we may find ourselves reacting to the new situation in precisely the same way as we reacted in the original relationship. Marian, for example, dared not disagree with her mother, however unreasonable she was being. If she did, she might forfeit her love. Thus Marian's insecurity and doubt about her self-worth increased over the years causing her to grow bitter. It was this insecurity and fear of contradicting that she brought into her relationship with Joy. She seemed stuck in a groove; fixed with child-like behaviour patterns.

Other people react to these transference experiences, the term used by psychologists to describe this unfortunate linking of the present with the past, in a totally different way. Instead of *repeating* the reactions of the past, they reverse them. So the curate who, from force of circumstances, was refused permission to challenge his authoritarian father even in his teenage years, may hit out, at least verbally, at his vicar if that vicar, the new authority figure in his life, does or says anything that even smacks of father and his regime. Or a youngster whose relationships with her parents or teachers have been full of nagging, criticism or hurt, may rebel in later life and hit out at any authority: the police, the boss at work, the government, or even the code of conduct generally accepted by society.

Repairing the rupture: evaluate

If friction between friends is to become a friend and not a foe, we must allow it to instruct us. We must evaluate. The following procedures, though not easy, are designed to result in an accurate, honest evaluation:

1. Take a step back from the relationship.
2. Pause before God.
3. Ask for a fresh touch from the Holy Spirit, the one whose role is to lead us into all truth (Jn 16:12).
4. Ask yourself, 'Have I ever encountered a situation like this before?'
5. Is there anything about this person that smacks of the past or a previous relationship? (Mannerisms, tone of voice, attitude to life, facial expression, eyes, gestures, method of conducting friendships.)
6. Am I relating only to this present friend or are there blurred edges: am I relating to ghosts of the past?
7. Are my reactions and the force of them consistent with what is going on in this friendship? Are they exaggerated?
8. Turn to the last chapter of this book and apply the 'seven E's' (page 189).

If you place your reactions under the microscope in this objective way, you might make clear connections between the past and the present, like Marian's link-up between Joy and her mother. In this event, there is no need to become introspective or despondent. That is unhealthy and harmful. No. Go to a wise Christian friend. Explain the situation. Ask them to pray for you. You are now on the threshold of an exhilarating discovery: that conflict is the nerve centre of growth.

Be healed

Express to your friend the hurt you first experienced in the original relationship. (Marian wept and wept as she recalled how crushed she had been by her mother's inability to express love to her in a way she could appreciate as a small girl.) Don't pretend the hurt isn't there. Jesus wants to heal it. Your friend, through prayer, and maybe the laying-on of hands, can pray with you that the Holy Spirit will touch and soothe and anoint the weeping sores, heal them over, bind up the broken parts of your spirit and make you whole.

When the healing balm of prayer is applied to our inner hurts, we lose the desire to carry round with us pockets of poison: the bitterness we once clutched to our breast like a priceless treasure, the resentment we clenched in our tight fist like the last possession we would relinquish to anyone. Healed and restored by Jesus, we are ready to let go of these hindrances. So the next stage is to pour out to Jesus, possibly in the presence of this same friend, pastor or counsellor, the full extent of your hostility. The abscess is thus lanced. The poison is drained away. And the blood of Jesus cleanses it from every vestige of sin. When we are thus released from the sin we have nursed, we let go of a burden. We are washed; made new. Whole.

Forgive

But there is yet more work to be done. Healed, cleansed, relieved, we must now obey the clear command of Jesus:

'Forgive'. We must not evade this. Rather, unhesitatingly and generously we must forgive the person who inflicted the pain in the first place and also forgive the person, who, in the present relationship, has been pressing, albeit un-wittingly, on past pain. What this means is that, in prayer, we must picture them wounding us. Look them in the eye. Say something like, 'It's really hurting. But just as the Lord has forgiven me, so I forgive you.'

Let go

Where that original hurting relationship was a parental one or a family or teacher-pupil one, it may be necessary to ask God to cut the cord that binds you to that person in an unhelpful way. An umbilical cord can feed a foetus or strangle it. Similarly, these relationships of the past may have contributed to our growth as adults or they may have stunted that growth. In any event, now God would set us free from them. We are to be in bondage to no one and nothing but him. Jesus is Lord. Let no one else, past or present, bring you into captivity. An important part of this ministry of prayer, then, is to ask Jesus to touch the memories of that past relationship so that they lose their power to sting or to cripple. Any unhelpful connections that still remain in your mind, your imagination or in your memory must be severed. Let go of them. This liberates you. You are now free from haunting fears of the past to begin the adventure of forging good friendships.

Conflict: a friend?

You may be free from fears of the past, but that is not to say you can freewheel into future friendships. The animosity that characterized Marian and Joy's friendship, just one example of fragmented friendships, left both of them bemused, bewildered and battered, like birds whose wings have been gummed up by an oil slick. They are free but not fully free. It takes time, patience and humility to so avail ourselves of the detergent of God's love that these bleeding wounds and squally relationships might be thoroughly cleansed by God. Healed. How, then, dare we call conflict a friend?

According to the writer of Proverbs, a friend is one whose wounds are faithful. In other words, a friend is one who notices anything amiss and reproves, rebukes and restores accordingly. That is why conflict, for Marian and Joy, was a friend. Conflict put its finger on unhealed areas in both of them (though there is no space here to unveil Joy's side of the story). Conflict's first friendly contribution is to confront me with the reality of the situation: I am not whole, I am imperfect, I still need to be transformed by God into the likeness of Jesus. What, then, is required if reconciliation is to take place?

Examine your expectations

First we must examine our original expectations of the friendship. We must also beware of imposing *our* expectations on the nature, degree and timing of God's healing. The resulting reconciliation must be God-designed, not man-manipulated. It could be that God will bring Marian and Joy back together again and enable them to relate as though nothing had happened to drive a wedge between them. What is more probable, and in such relationships often more necessary, is that both must learn to renegotiate the friendship on a new set of terms.

Renegotiate the friendship on a new set of terms

In order to do this some soul-searching questions need to be asked:

1. How appropriate was it that we expected closeness, the togetherness of two fingers coexisting on the same hand? Was that God's plan for our friendship?

2. Are there certain hopes and expectations of this friendship that we must now willingly sacrifice, either because they are unattainable or because God seems to be redirecting our lives?
3. Are we willing to co-operate as parts of the body of Christ, not like two fingers sharing the same hand, but with the space enjoyed, for example, by a knee cap and a thumb?
4. Are we trying to cling to a friendship God never intended for us, or are we prepared to become to each other the friends *God* always wanted us to be?
5. Can I hold this friendship, not in a tightly clenched fist, but on the open palm of my hand—to be removed or restored as God chooses?

To let go of cherished hopes, expectations and friendships involves disappointment and pain. Disappointment is rather like bereavement. It is characterized by sorrow, loss and emptiness. Invite God into the void. He is the available God, God-with-us, who identifies with our pain. Peel off the garments of self-pity. Clothe yourself continually with the Holy Spirit's armour which alone will equip you in your battle with despair, feelings of failure and remorse.

Fight

Free from the fears of the past, you are free now to fight. We must fight the real enemy, which is not the friend with whom you are locked in conflict, but, as we saw in Chapter 1, the evil one, Satan, and the evil that lurks within and that keeps you from loving others with a Christlike love. In Ephesians 6.11ff., Paul instructs us how to fight. He issues a curt command: appropriate every piece of the spiritual armour provided by God.

This is vital, because when conflict beats friendship in the same way as waves crash against cliffs in a storm, Satan is never far away. He condemns. He accuses. He lies. And he confuses. We must be aware of his tactics and be ever on-guard. Moreover, we must be clad in the armour which is not as cumbersome as the physical, military equipment described by Paul but which is, in short, Jesus himself. What Paul is implying in Ephesians 6 is, put on Jesus in the same way as people put on warm clothes when they venture out in winter. Protect every possible part of yourself with Jesus. In the aftermath of conflict this is strengthening.

Satan will delight to remind you of the row you had with your friend and will whisper accusing words, 'Failure, hypocrite', in your ear. Instead of believing his lying tongue, strap round yourself the belt of truth (the living word, Jesus). Wield the sword of the Spirit (the written word of God). Remind Satan that, like Jesus, these God facts control your life, not the devil's weird whispers that come without warning.

Similarly, Satan will wound your emotions. He delights to cause confusion by churning Christians' feelings. We need not capitulate. Instead, we can place the breastplate and the shield (Jesus himself) between Satan's flame-tipped arrow and ourselves. Thus we shall know ourselves encircled by Christ and his love. Completely protected.

When Satan distorts our thinking, as he will try to, we will place on our heads the helmet of salvation. Jesus. We will remind Satan that we have resolved to live biblically, that we are in submission to King Jesus, that his word rules our lives.

Thus equipped by the enfolding of Jesus and by our obedience to him, Satan and self do not stand a chance. They retreat, defeated because we stand on and live in the victory of Jesus. I am not pretending this is easy. I am saying it is possible.

Prayer

Part of the warfare against the evil that is present in all conflict is the weapon of prayer. Faced with conflict, we must pray with perseverance, that is, until the relationship is brought into alignment with God's will. We must pray

alongside the Man of Prayer, Jesus, praying that our friendships will be purged of sin. We must pray against the
principalities and powers who seek to obstruct God's
answers to these prayers (Dan 10:10–13). We must be on
the alert when we pray: see prayer as an essential part of the
battle. We must pray always (Eph 6:18). And we must
recognize that prayer is a paradox. As St Augustine put it:
'I will pray as though everything depended on God. I will
work as though everything depended on me.' This work
includes praying for the one who has hurt or offended us. It
means praying for reconciliation. It involves praying that,
ultimately, God's will may be accomplished. In addition, it
is sometimes necessary to invite one or two trusted friends
to hold the untidy tangle into the reconciling love of God on
our behalf. And, of course, we must always be ready to
become the answers to our own prayers by forgiving, taking
risks, submitting ourselves to the transforming love of God
and concentrating more on the things that unite us as
members of the body of Christ than the things that divide.

Confess and forgive

Friendship Jesus-style is characterized by unfailing forgiveness. When your friend has failed you, hurt you yet again,
don't brush it under the carpet, pretending it hasn't
happened. Acknowledge the hurt. Feel the full force of the
pain. Then, in prayer, stand with your friend at the foot of
Christ's cross. Look him in the eye, as it were, as I said
before. Tell him that it really hurts, but let your love extend
beyond the pain. Forgive him freely. This is forgiveness
Jesus-style: love embracing the hurt *and* the one who cause
the injury; love continuing to express itself actively and
with compassion.

Such love is slow to apportion blame, as Paul reminds us
in 1 Corinthians 13:4–7; it is, however, quick to admit
personal culpability. The reason why fractures in friendship
often fester is that one or both parties refuse to admit that

even a portion of the blame might be theirs. This is tragic. Admit your own failure before God. Don't grovel. Do confess—first to God, then to your friend. Having acknowledged your own failure, perhaps with that powerful little word-trio, *I am sorry*, ask your friend a direct question, 'Will you forgive me?' I have on my desk a card from a friend to whom I put that question recently. Her warm response *'Of course,* I'll forgive you' brings healing to some very grazed places inside of me and motivates me to work towards lasting reconciliation.

Take risks Jesus-style

While this undercurrent of prayer, forgiveness and an openness to the miracle of reconciliation gains momentum, which may take months, we must also model our lives on the pattern established for us by Jesus. Conflict is the friend who places his finger on blemishes in our lives that need to be dealt with. Conflict is also the counsellor who shows us the need to renegotiate a certain relationship on a new set of terms. Conflict between friends frequently brings them into a no-man's-land, the place between the relationship as it was and the relationship as it will become.

It is all too easy, while we lie low in this no-man's-land, to withdraw, to freeze, to avoid the former friend's gaze, to watch where they sit in church on Sunday and sit as far away as possible. This defensive detachment is understandable; it is a frightening experience to feel your entire body stiffen when one you used to care about comes into a room. Such avoidance is understandable but *un*biblical.

Jesus' friendships were sometimes stormy too but he refused to withdraw into a hedgehog ball. Instead, as John shows, he set himself up for more rejection and hurt (Jn 6:60–70). When Jesus watched his disciples take offence at his teaching and abandon him, he turned to the twelve with the question, 'You do not want to leave too, do you?' Peter vowed loyalty at that moment only to stab him with the knife-wound of rejection later.

If we would offer friendship Jesus-style, even when the going is tough and former friends have deserted us, we must be prepared to take the risk: to reach out to offer continued friendship fully recognizing that this might be flung back in our face. This is the commitment Jesus models to us.

Count the cost

We began this chapter by examining the value of friend-ship. We must conclude it by coming to terms with reality. True friendship is costly. Your friend is imperfect. You are imperfect. Ask two imperfects to create a close relationship and the result is inevitable pain. In close friendships pain is guaranteed. Those who shrink from pain will shrink from intimacy also. Only those who will face their fears and fractured friendships with Christ will flourish in the commitment of shared love.

Give thanks

The conflict that brought Marian to near-despair resulted in prolific personal growth. God came into the hurts she had concealed since she was a little girl and healed them. He forgave her for the bitterness she had harboured against her mother and enabled her to forgive her for the unintentional harm she had caused. The old ties that kept Marian bound to childish behaviour patterns when in her mother's presence were cut. And Marian reclothed herself in God's spiritual armour as she prepared to venture prayerfully into the future: to relate anew to her mother and to Joy. That is not to say the friendship with Joy repaired easily or immediately. It often happens in such situations that two people grope back to one another slowly and cautiously and this is often wise.

But Marian bounced up to me the other day. Her eyes

sparkled and her smile was bright as the news bubbled out of her. 'My mother's just spent the week with us. It was a lovely time. We spent hours and hours just talking to each other. She came to church with us and began asking lots of questions about the Lord. . .'

As I walked away from Marian that night, I thanked God for her conflict: the beauty that rises from its ashes when the chaos is handed to him. I reflected on Marian's growth. Unless conflict had driven a wedge between her and Joy, Marian's relationship with her mother might never have been restored. Unless Marian had stumbled through the dark tunnel of conflict, she might never have sought prayer ministry for personal healing; never tasted the wine that is the produce of the crushed grape. Conflict, for Marian, had indeed become the nerve centre of growth.

4

When Friends Fight

The deeper I journey into this book, the more aware I
become of fractured friendships. Of course, my antennae
are out: alert, tuned into any situation that might have
relevance to this book. But I am not having to look far.
Most days, it seems, I pick up the telephone only to hear of
more conflict tearing members of the church fellowship
apart. I talk to my husband only to detect rumblings of
conflict threatening to disrupt the staff team. And, yes, alas!
I cannot ignore the seeds of this selfsame conflict germina-
ting in myself also. There is no getting away from it. Conflict
is all around us. It sometimes seems, as I write this book, as
though I am wading knee-deep in its black, unsavoury
sludge.

In this chapter, we continue our examination of fractured
friendships and search for an answer to two basic
questions. 'What causes fighting between friends?' 'How
can we handle these heartbreak situations lovingly and
wisely?'

Why friends fight: self-centredness

We saw in the first chapter of this book that one of the
reasons why conflict erupts is that though we are Christians,

self has not died but is very much alive. This self rampages like a wild beast when it cannot have its own way or when it is hurt. This rebellious, self-pitying, self-assertive 'me' is at the core of disruptive friendships. When it is hurt or dismayed or disgruntled it gives vent to its feelings even when the well-being of others is endangered. It leaves a trail of destruction in its wake.

This has become a serious problem between friends because there is a philosophy now widely believed even by Christians that a person has a right to ventilate his feelings, however dark or negative they may be. Indeed, we are told that such dustbin-tipping is essential to our emotional health. The propaganda goes further. It persuades us that what we *feel* is objective truth. In other words, if I feel you have let me down, this proves that you have let me down. Such a philosophy, of course, is nonsense. But many of us imbibe this teaching unquestioningly. So if I feel my friend has betrayed me, I accuse him. I even believe it is my right to do so. By labelling him with a name like 'traitor', I not only confine him to a restrictive pigeon-hole, I withdraw my trust; and worse, I pour onto him the full force of my wrath. And I wonder why the friendship-boat lies on the rocks, wrecked.

Uncontrolled anger

This self-centred, uncontrolled behaviour is un-Christlike and unbiblical. Yet such worldly philosophy has become the life-principle of some Christians. They have ignored the fact that the Christian should take as his yardstick only the behavioural standards that are consistent with life in the kingdom of God: the kingdom of love. They have ignored the fact that, if Jesus is Lord, feelings must never be given permission to dominate a person's life. They have ignored the fact that love takes responsibility for others, never thinks primarily of its own needs, however urgent they may be, never demands its own way. They have ignored Paul's teaching: Love 'is not irritable or touchy. It does not hold grudges and will hardly even notice when others do it wrong.... If you love someone you will be loyal to him no matter what the cost' (1 Cor 13:5, 7, TLB).

Because this teaching has been laid on one side, what often happens between Christians is this. One is angry with another. He picks up the phone on impulse and gives vent to his anger without stopping to ask what damage the onslaught might do.

The damage this thoughtlessness creates was underlined for me on one occasion when my husband and I were invited out to dinner by a friend. We had scarcely crossed his threshold when the torrent of abuse began: 'You really let me down at the committee meeting last night. You made me look pretty stupid and I've got to be honest with you, I'm still hopping mad.'

The result of this 'welcome' was a tense start to a dinner party we had hoped to enjoy. This kind of behaviour is un-Christlike. It is the antithesis of speaking the truth in love (Eph 4:15). It prises Christians apart.

Jealousy

Another reason why friends fight is that, even though we are Christians and even though we know in our heads that this means that we are each uniquely usable by God, we are still insecure, pygmy people. We are rather like children playing on the nursery floor: never content with the toy God has given us to play with but always looking over our shoulder at our friends' toys, coveting them. If God or our friend refuses to comply with our whims and wishes, we throw a tantrum. Translate that into adult terms and you are left with one word: jealousy.

Jealousy is looking out of the corner of your eye at your friend's personality or looks or possessions or talents and bemoaning, albeit only to yourself, 'It's not fair...'. The discontentment that is an inevitable strand of jealousy frequently results in rivalry, the competitive spirit that destroys good friendships; in short, conflict. Such jealousy rose up in a friend of mine on one occasion. A member of the household where he lived, John, was invited to lead a group in his church, a group that my friend had hoped to lead himself. Resentment raged inside him like a forest fire that refused to be extinguished. 'Why haven't I been chosen to do that job? Why have they handpicked John? I know I could do the job better than him. Besides, I'm much more prayerful than he is and I'm much more experienced.'

Jealousy turned in upon itself festers and results in the discontentment which resents God for being big enough and creative enough to make a vast variety of one-off personality moulds. Christian communities, families and friendships find it hard to survive in the wake of such conflicting emotions.

Displacement

Another reason why friendships fracture is that friendships must change as circumstances change. We all know that with our minds but when we translate it into experience and change becomes synonymous with displacement, we become anxious, fearful, sometimes even bitter and angry. The disappointment that accompanies such displacement can result in depression.

Chris and Simon

This happened to Chris. Chris and her brother, Simon were students at the same university. Neither wanted to live in the halls of residence so they shared a flat. They each forged new friendships. Even so, a large proportion of their leisure time was spent together. They both became Christians at the same time and joined a lively church together. Their brother-sister friendship was supportive and good.

Then Simon fell head over heels in love. Simon had never

dared to hope that a girl would even look at him. But now Jane had fallen for him and he couldn't get her out of his mind. They spent every possible moment together: even started having breakfast together. 'We really want to get to know each other...'

And Chris became more and more withdrawn as life for her became increasingly lonely. Eventually, she went to her doctor who prescribed anti-depressants. Chris was relieved that these blocked out the pain of rejection which was too hard for her to handle on her own

Chris had known, of course, that one day this could happen; that one day she might have to stand aside and watch Simon relate more closely to another girl. Chris was generous. She was glad for them; gave thanks sincerely when she saw their happiness and felt guilty that she missed Simon's companionship. Chris even condemned herself for feeling lonely. Thus she stumbled deeper and deeper into the pitch-black tunnel of depression. If Simon did decide to spend time in the flat, she would avoid him, not wanting the dreariness of her feelings to spoil his happiness. And there was no one she would talk to.

Such displacement can feel frightening until we have established a new routine; until we have given ourselves time and space to work out how we are going to venture into the next phase of life without the accustomed friend or companion. Such displacement gives birth to unspoken hostility.

Hidden hostilities are as much a sign of conflict as flare-ups and as potentially destructive. Like all conflict, they can also be growth-inducing as we shall go on to observe later in this chapter.

Exclusiveness

Simon and Jane's behaviour was neither sensitive nor Christlike. The exclusiveness they indulged in blighted Chris's life. Indeed it seemed like a form of torture.

That is not to say that people in love should refrain from spending time together alone. Of course not. Lovers must create around themselves a space in which their love and understanding of one another can grow and flourish. But it does say that where lovers or friends are so absorbed in one another that they neglect and abandon former friends in the same way as they discarded their love-battered friend of childhood, the Teddy bear, then self-indulgence and self-centredness need to be confessed and dispensed with. Such cruelty should find no place in the Christian's conduct. It is one of the causes of conflict between Christians. Another contributing cause is possessiveness.

Possessiveness

Margaret Evening makes a shrewd observation about the possessiveness that erodes many relationships. 'As soon as one friend becomes possessive towards another, the death-knell of that relationship has begun to toll. For possessiveness confines and encloses, till like a moth in a jam jar, the "other" bats his wings to break loose and be free again' (*Who Walk Alone,* Hodder & Stoughton, 1974, p.44).

Ian and Tim

Ian and Tim helped me to realize the truth of this claim. They were students together when their friendship first sprang to life. When they moved from university to a city where they knew no one, their friendship seemed to take on a new dimension. They needed each other. The friendship deepened.

Over the months, they began to express their dependency on each other and affection for one another in physical ways: hugging, cuddling, kissing. It was a short step from there to indulge in homosexual genital play. Eventually guilt set in and they came to ask for help.

Tim described the friendship from which he wanted to

escape. It had become, to use Henri Nouwen's words, 'needy and greedy, sticky and clinging, dependent and sentimental, exploitative and parasitic'—in short, unhealthy and sin-based. Clearly the friendship had either to fold up or be renegotiated on a new set of terms. Until this occurred, frequent quarrels and an undercurrent of conflict would continue to characterize the relationship.

When one friend tries to possess another, either emotionally or spiritually, let alone sexually, conflict is bound to erupt. When someone possesses us, they place us in bondage. But in Christ we are free—not slaves. We are to be in bondage to nothing and no one except Jesus, the Lord.

You can tell whether exclusiveness and possessiveness is threatening your friendships by applying certain questions to them:

1. Are other people welcomed or resented?
2. Does the presence of others evoke jealousy?
3. Does the friendship consume an inordinate amount of time: time spent together, time spent fantasizing about the friendship, time wasted anticipating future times together? Does time apart from the friend(s) seem frustrating, boring, wasted?
4. Does the prospect of separation from the friend or a lessening of intensity or intimacy fill you with dread?

Where the answer to these questions is yes, it is a certain sign that the dynamics of the relationship need to change. More space is vital.

Claustrophobic closeness

Claustrophobic closeness ruins relationships. It contributes to conflict. Friends must give one another space to move away from each other, space to move towards others, space to grow into God, and space to move towards each other again. Cramp your friend's space and he will move away from you. Clutter his space with your persistent and pressing

needs, and he will flee. Crowd the friendship with claustrophobic and Messianic expectations and the relationship will
crumble, like a wall that was never constructed to bear such
a load. But unclench your fists, set your friend free, and he
will move back to you. It is a mystery: a paradox. A great
deal of unexpressed animosity among friends exists because
one is demanding of the other more than the friend can
hope to give.

Personality clash

But the reaons why some friends fight has nothing to do
with the subtleties I have mentioned so far. It is far more
straightforward than that. They have been created by God
with distinct differences. They are opposites in everything:
tastes, personalities, behaviour, outlook, habits. They clash.

The conflict that erupts between opposite and opposing
personalities is the most spectacular of all. The clash
happens with all the explosiveness and vigour of a firework
display. It happened between Jill and Barbara when they
attempted to share a flat. Jill was bouncy, gregarious, loved
to entertain. Barbara was quiet, meditative and loved long
evenings in the quietness of her own room. The clash was
predictable—but painful. And so was the confrontation
that was the inevitable climax of the personality clash driving
both Pete and Leslie demented. They, too, shared a flat.
Pete was fastidious, obsessional about tidiness, a fanatic
about health hygiene. Leslie, on the other hand, just took
life as it came. 'Why wash up every day when once a week
will do? Why put clothes away as long as you know where
they are?'

You can do two things with such conflict: despair or
learn. We must learn how such situations can be used to
make us more loving and more wise. We look, now, at how
this worked in some of the situations I have mentioned.

Make conflict work for you: grow in self-awareness

Take the frozen welcome my husband and I once received from the friend I mentioned earlier in this chapter, for example. I felt offended by his comments. Still smarting, I eventually asked God, 'Lord, what was it about me which found it hard to receive his anger?' I became aware of my own selfishness. I had expected the evening in his home to be about *receiving* support. I should have been generous enough and loving enough to go equipped to *offer* support so that we could enjoy mutuality, so that his wounding comments had no power to hurt.

And God showed me another home truth. There are times when I, too, ventilate anger. It seems to spill out, like lava pouring from a volcano. Jesus seemed to be challenging *me*: 'Has it ever occurred to you to stop and to question whether others can take your wrath at this moment or in this place or expressed in this way?' Before the all-searching eye of God, I felt small, worm-like. He knows perfectly well that those questions rarely occur to me when *I* consider *I* have a right to express anger. Yet, I was expecting of my friend a standard of behaviour that I do not impose upon myself. Jesus has a word for this: hypocrite.

Yes, conflict is the friend that wounds, the counsellor determined to reflect back to us what we are really like, the one desiring to promote our growth. Not all such growth is comfortable or easy. Much of it is costly. Some of it is produced by tension and struggle. But just as wild cyclamen in Cyprus strain every fibre to push their way through tiny crevices in rocks and flower there, so we must strain every nerve to grow through conflict. When Jesus uses conflict to confront us with our own un-Christlikeness, conflict becomes a caring companion whom we cannot ignore because our goal in life is to become imitators of Christ.

Grow in 'other' awareness

Through conflict, Christ may confront us with our own hypocrisy. Through conflict he may also open our eyes to see the wonder of the variety most of us applaud in nature yet despise when someone's 'otherness' threatens me.

The phone rang last night. The caller was the young man I mentioned earlier in this chapter who used to be eaten-up by jealousy because another member of his household, John, had been chosen to lead a group in preference to him.

'The group went really well tonight, Joyce. John led it superbly.'

What has brought about this change in attitude? How has jealousy been converted into appreciation?

Over the months, this young Christian, confronted by conflict, has worked through the frustration, asking God to change *him*. He placed jealousy and pride at the foot of the cross to be purged by God. He exposed the insecurities and hurts at the root of the jealousy to God's healing touch. He learned to value himself as a person with a unique contribution to make towards God's kingdom. He no longer feels threatened by John. Instead, he recognizes that John's gifts are different, 'other', complementary to his own. He appreciates John and is generous enough to tell him so.

Two questions came frequently to this young man's lips while he was attending to the jealousy, treating his conflict as an assignment to be worked at:

Lord, what is it about me that cannot cope with the situation?
Lord, how do you want to transform me so that I am more like you in my behaviour?

These vital, perennial questions must be asked if, for us, conflict is to become, not the nerve-shattering, last straw that precipitates a breakdown, but the nerve-strengthening phenomenon that results in a spurt of growth.

Acceptance

Conflict taught this young man the miracle-working power of free and fearless acceptance. By acceptance I mean the generosity of spirit that recognizes another person as an individual in his own right. By acceptance I mean the desire to understand, value and affirm his uniqueness. By acceptance I mean the determination truly to serve and love him. It was conflict with John which taught my friend how to do this. The experience was liberating.

When we accept a person, instead of feeling threatened by his differences, we glory in his 'otherness'. We see the person as someone who is perfectly at liberty to disagree with us, challenge us, reject our plans and repudiate our views. We grant the other freedom to stand up for himself if necessary. It is conflict which pushes us into the cleft-stick crises where we have to decide: 'Will I offer such acceptance, genuine recognition of worth and affirmation, or will I withhold it?' When we open our hearts to another, we facilitate his growth and our own, eliminate the sting of loneliness, banish friction and become free to acknowledge our own worth.

Avoid exclusiveness

Such acceptance brings an inevitable closeness between two or more people. Simon and Jane enjoyed this oneness and so did Ian and Tim. This closeness is one of the rich rewards of friendship for the persons concerned. It can be communicated non-verbally: by a glance, a knowing look, a shared giggle. This unspoken language is fun, even healing, for the persons concerned. The problem is that these audible and visible embodiments of mutual understanding communicate a clear message to those outside the friendship: you are not included in this; you are on the fringe of our relationship. This was the message Simon and Jane conveyed to Chris and it wounded her deeply.

But the pain and conflict was not wasted. When Chris eventually crawled out of the tunnel of depression, she acknowledged that she was stronger and wiser as a person because of the inner turmoil. She even believed that God had allowed the experience to wean her away from over-dependence on Simon so that she could renew her dependence on Jesus.

Chris also learned that, however close you are to someone, however special they are to you and you to them, however vulnerable you have been to one another, friends do not possess each other. Neither do they belong exclusively to each other. Exclusive belonging exists in marriage, not in friendship. Friends must, therefore, give one another space; they may even have to let one another go.

It was conflict which put its finger on this painful yet liberating truth for Chris. She not only learned the lesson but acted on it. She not only let Simon go, she took the risk and began to forge new friendships, thus becoming a more whole and integrated person.

And she carried another insight into these friendships: the fact that, though friendship in one sense excludes others by its very nature of clubbableness and shared interests, at the same time friends must always be prepared to include others, for friendship ceases to become innocent when it weaves around itself a web which keeps others out.

Commitment

As Chris took these lessons on board, healing came and she recommitted herself to her brother. Such commitment is one of the ingredients of firm friendship. 'I say I'll be your friend, I'll always be your friend.'

We, too, need this leavening ingredient of love. Its presence ensures that even when conflict erupts, the friends will reaffirm their friendship because, deep down, they both believe: 'We matter to each other. We are in this together. We are going to make this conflict work *for* us and not allow it to divide us.' Its presence ensures that the hurts inflicted by conflict are not just ignored, but healed. Its presence persuades friends in the belief that God is bigger than the mistakes we make in relationships; that he even weaves these mistakes into the tapestry that is friendship.

As for Chris and Simon, they are reconciled now, discovering the truth of an observation made to me by a friend with whom I had quarrelled: 'Quarrels between friends are for making up.' It is my experience that the making-up is sweet.

5

Hostility in the Home

Lack of hostility in the home depends not so much on the people you live with as the person *you are*; on the kind of person you are becoming. Few of us like to acknowledge this challenging fact. Nevertheless, it is a sobering truth that when I allow God to touch and transform my attitude and behaviour, tensions in the home die down. Some even disappear instantly. In Chapter 6 we shall examine how this applies to relationships within the nuclear family. In this chapter, we focus on the community and on the extended family where parents, children and others live together. I use the word community with two concepts in mind. First, meaning groups or pairs of friends who choose to share a flat or a house. Second, meaning groups of Christians who have committed themselves to one another to share a common life either for a limited period of time or for life. In this chapter, then, three basic questions must occupy our minds: Why does conflict erupt in community and in the extended family? How should such conflict be handled? How may these clashes be so resolved that they become constructive rather than destructive?

Why conflict erupts: blaming

'I'm tired of being woken up every morning by a baby that isn't my own and I'm really fed up with forever tripping over toddler's toys when that toddler isn't mine.' The speaker was Sue, a member of a Christian community.

'I really don't know if I can share a flat with Len much longer. I think he's disgusting. You should see the fat spilling down the cooker. It looks like well-set candle wax it's been there for so long. And as for the grill pan, he never thinks of washing it even though he cooks bacon and sausages for breakfast every morning.' The speaker was Roger, a friend of mine, whose intolerance for his flatmate grew week by week until eventually he left.

'Life at home's become unbearable since my gran moved in. She fusses over me as though I'm a little girl. She thinks I should be in by ten every night. She can't bear it if even faint strains of my radio reach her ears but she turns *her* television set up full volume. And she's so demanding of my time; always expecting me to sit in her room and talk to her.' This speaker was Felicity, a twenty-year-old, whose resentment of her grandmother's presence in the home was souring many relationships.

Notice the common thread running through these complaints. Blaming. When hostility hangs over the home like a thunder-cloud, most of us look for someone to blame; someone, anyone, other than ourselves, at whom to point the finger. Most of us refuse to acknowledge that *we* are blameworthy or that we must shoulder at least a portion of the blame. This results in bitterness and the despondency that causes us to withdraw from one another. Several factors contribute to this blame-attaching syndrome.

Inadequate preparations

One reason why conflict in community flares up with such frightening ferocity is that certain essential preparations have never been made. I am not talking now about practical preparations, like the creation of a specially designed 'granny flat', important as these are, but of preparing for the emotional adjustments, which are just as important as the practical ones.

Whenever Christians propose to create an extended family, or to join one, changes in lifestyle are required of all the persons concerned. In any transition of this kind, there is joy and pain; there are hopes and there are fears. Each person should acknowledge their hopes. 'What am I hoping for from this new set-up?' It often helps to record these hopes in writing. Each person must come to terms with their fears. 'What is the worst that can happen if this arrangement doesn't work out? What other fears lurk in the shadows of my mind?' Write the fears alongside the hopes. Each person must be realistic. Tell God your expectations. Tell him your dreads. Go further. Ask him to put his finger on habits or attitudes in *you* that might hinder good relationships with those with whom you are about to share a home: Perhaps you leave little piles of smelly socks on the bathroom floor after you've washed? Perhaps you are pernickety, insisting the washing-up is done immediately? Maybe you are insensitive to others' needs for quiet or solitude? Maybe it never occurs to you to wash the bath after you've used it? Or perhaps you are fastidious about layers of dust settling on the skirting boards? Give God an opportunity to put his finger on *your* habits or *your* attitudes. Allow him to change them for the sake of the well-being of others who will soon be part of your household.

Lack of clarification

You are not the only person who holds on to hopes and fears as you move into this household. Each person who will be calling this house 'home' also harbours hopes, expectations, longings and dreads. These must be placed alongside your own. The two sets must be examined carefully. One of the reasons why communities of Christians collapse, with all the attending heartache, is that, in establishing the household, they applied over-spiritual rather than realistic criteria. They made the bold but inaccurate assumption: 'We're all Christians. We're bound to get on.' Experiences like the ones I quoted at the beginning of this chapter illustrate that this assumption is far from the truth. No Christian Utopia where friends 'live together happily ever after' exists this side of eternity. If Christian relationships are to work they have to be worked at. The minimum requirements of each member of the household must be recognized and met.

Crossed wires

If Christians are to be honest with one another in an attempt to protect the home from unnecessary hostility, each person must learn the difficult art of communication. As we saw in Chapter 2, this is a two-pronged activity. It involves transmitting a single message verbally and non-verbally. It also involves accurate listening. Accurate listening is the ability to hear what someone else is really saying rather than so filtering whatever we hear through our own hurts, insecurities and prejudices that we distort or change the message completely. Belinda and her mother find it very hard to do this.

Belinda is in her twenties. She loves shampooing and blow-drying people's hair. Her mother was ill and depressed when I overheard this conversation:

'Hi, Mum! How're you feeling?'

'Not too bad, Belinda, thank you.'

'D'you want me to get you something to eat? How about an omelette?'

'No, thank you, dear. I'm not hungry.'

Belinda made several similar attempts to cheer her mother up:

'When d'you want me to wash your hair then? I haven't done it for over a week.'

'Oh Belinda! Don't be so rude. I know I look like an old hag. But there's no need to nag and criticize me. You know I'm not well. Why can't you leave me alone. My hair can wait for another few days surely?'

'Oh! Sorry I spoke. I was only trying to be helpful. Why d'you always twist everything I say? I thought you'd feel better if your hair looked nice. I thought you *liked* me doing it.'

This kind of twisted communication that causes us such agony and that, I suspect, causes Satan much mirth, frequently causes friction in the home. You think you are making a straightforward statement: 'I'd like to make you feel better by washing your hair.' You know exactly what you are trying to communicate. Somehow in the space that lies between your lips and another's mind, the words become distorted or confused. A member of the household might hear you say something quite different from the words you articulated: 'How dare you call me an old hag?'

Lack of encouragement

Another reason why hostility divides households is that Christians fail to encourage one another; neglect to express appreciation of each other. Instead, they fall prey to criticizing, backbiting, accusing and, that creeping disease common to most communities, gossip.

Think back to the illustrations I used at the beginning of this chapter. Sue and Felicity were both full of animosity towards others in their household. And so was Len's flatmate, Roger. But Len had opened his home to Roger at cost to himself, when his now-embittered flatmate had been homeless. Roger had forgotten this fact.

Paul speaks against the negativism that pervades all-too-many households. There must be no such things as quarrels and jealousies (Rom 13:13). Instead, 'Do everything possible to live in peace with everybody' (Rom 12:18).

Self-centredness

Another contributing cause of conflict in community is the innate selfishness of each individual. It is tempting to wonder when moving into a community or extended family 'What's in it for me?' This attitude is worldy; unbiblical. But it lay at the root of Sue's disillusionment with Christian community. It also prevented Roger from settling into Len's flat peaceably.

Again, it is the apostle Paul who challenges this attitude. Christians are to consider others 'better than themselves', that is, to consider others 'their betters'. In other words, Paul implies, 'Don't first ask, "How can everyone else meet my needs or pamper me?" Rather, inquire, "How can I serve others?"' This is the prevailing attitude that should be the mainspring of all our activity within the community. But let us not be naïve. Even when all the members of the household keep this goal before them, friction will not disappear. What will happen is that the level of friction will be considerably reduced.

The neglect of love

Love assumes responsibility for the loved one. Yet another reason why Christians fail in their attempt to set up home together is that they fail to assume responsibility for one another. By this, I mean they fail to so listen to one another that they enter the other's world, view life through the other's spectacles, put themselves in the other's shoes. If both Felicity and her grandmother had done this, the effect would have been similar to opening the window of a stuffy bedroom on a day in spring. If both Len and Roger had done this, the effect would have been like sweeping the garden path clear of autumn leaves.

Most communities fall far short of Jesus' love standard. He took responsibility for his friends by caring for them, recognizing even their unspoken needs, and meeting them.

He relaxed with them and prayed with them. That is why they enjoyed such a high level of togetherness.

Not enough space

If members of the household are to enjoy similar warmth and togetherness—the openness that reveals secret hopes and fears, the mask-removing that unveils failures and intolerable burdens, the childlikeness that is unafraid to have fun—then they must also set limits on this togetherness and preserve their personal space. If they fail in this task, eventually hostilities will multiply and wound.

Space is as essential to relationships as the gap between rungs of the ladder. Shared lives within fixed boundaries spells security. Shared lives stripped of such separateness spells, at best an exposure from which one party will eventually run, at worst, an unhealthy bondage where two or more people are held together by the confidentiality of secrets shared. As Henri Nouwen puts it, 'Space can only be a welcoming space when there are clear boundaries' (*Reaching Out,* Fount, 1975, p.91).

Fear of confrontation

If each person's privacy is to be thus preserved, and if the individual's pressing needs are to be met realistically, the art of sensitive confrontation must be learned by each member of the household. Some Christians fear the very word confrontation. It conjures up ugly images: a head-on collision, a ding-dong battle, cruel clashing of personalities and views, angry outbursts, wounding experiences. Thus Sue refrained from voicing her resentment about the toddler's toys and though Roger grumbled to *me* about the fat on the cooker, he never even mentioned it to Len.

This fear of confrontation is regrettable. It results in resentment and the hard-heartedness that divides. And it is not Christlike. As we shall go on to observe, Jesus was confrontational as a person without stooping to becoming an argumentative person. In this, as in everything, Jesus is to be our model.

We have observed some of the reasons why conflict erupts in households and communities. We must now move on to consider how such conflict can be avoided.

Coping with conflict: examine your expectations

Before Christians move in together, it is wise to respond to some basic questions:

1. What am I hoping for from this household or community in terms of friendship and fellowship?
2. Shall we pray together? How often?
3. How much time shall we spend together?
4. How will *you* feel if I go out with my friends and you are in alone?
5. What shall we do about cooking—have a rota, do it when we feel like it, or what?
6. Who will do the cleaning, hoovering, washing, ironing, shopping?
7. How shall we pay the telephone bills?
8. Are there any habits or attitudes of mine that you know of which you find particularly irritating?

Each individual should take a careful look at their personal response to these questions. These must be placed alongside the response of the others proposing to share the home. Where you bring similar hopes and expectations, problems will be minimal. The differences are the potentially divisive factors.

For example, it might happen that two people sharing the same flat decide to pray together. One might want this shared prayer to take place every day. The other might find it too time-consuming, too demanding. In such an eventuality, a satisfactory middle course must be found. For the sake of unity and the well-being of all concerned, each person might need to adjust their initial preference so that each person's need is met. Blaming and criticizing must be shed like outworn garments. In their place, each person must put the needs of the others before their own. Where each person of a Christian household does this, and such a high standard of self-sacrifice needs to be a *shared* activity, conflict has little hope of creating lasting havoc.

There is also value in setting aside a regular time for reviewing hopes and expectations after the initial settling-in period. This should be a time, perhaps monthly or bi-monthly, when each person examines early hopes and new expectations and when the following questions might be used as a basis for evaluation:

1. How far are my hopes being fulfilled?
2. Where I am disappointed, is it because I am being unrealistic or because we are not achieving our potential?
3. I feel disappointed because...Is there a solution to this problem?
4. How can we work at it together?

Such discussions are of value, of course, only if all parties concerned are prepared to be honest and to change or prune their hopes and expectations where these prove to be unrealistic or self-centred. The task in hand is to ensure that each person's needs are met but that this need-meeting slots into the hopes and expectations of the others with the ease and strength of a mitred corner on a picture frame. In relationships, such joins need frequent adjusting if they are to be kept firm and sweet and if unnecessary conflict is to be avoided.

Clarify

Belinda and her mother, whom I mentioned earlier in this chapter, discovered how easily conflict arises through mis-understanding. This happens in extended households and communities also. The clue is to clarify. In the face of such misunderstanding, it is wise to enquire, 'What do you think

I said?' or 'What did you hear me say?' Patience is vital at this stage. It may be as necessary to repeat or rephrase your original statement to a certain member of the household as it is when speaking to a person with impaired hearing; to spell out the message with clarity, care, compassion and gentleness and to double-check that they have heard what you intended to say.

Encourage

Hostility sometimes seems to claw at Christian communities and households like an angry dog scratching at a closed door. Such hostility need not destroy the home as long as the real situation is acknowledged: that each person who forms a part of this household is less than perfect. Like us, they were born with a bias, not to obey God, but to disobey him. They may be Christians but they are not stained-glass-window saints. The flaws and eccentricities of others must not be ignored, but they must not be magnified either. If we remember this, whenever we see others struggling to follow the pattern of Jesus for at least part of the day, we will give silent thanks to God for this manifestation of his indwelling presence and grace. From time to time we will reflect this back to the person concerned in the form of appreciation and encouragement. In this way, we motivate others to submit themselves to being changed by the Holy Spirit of God. An ounce of appreciation is worth more than a ton of criticism. A drop of encouragement goes further than a bucketful of criticism. One 'well done' dropped into the domestic pool results in joy spreading through the entire household. Affirmation keeps relationships in good working order and dispels tension.

Become like Jesus—a servant

We saw earlier in this chapter, as well as in a previous one, that self-assertion is a tyrant. When we lay on one side the

'What's in it for me?' mentality and substitute it with questions like 'What can I contribute to these people to whom I'm committed?' old values are turned on their head. Pleasant surprises await us. It no longer matters that toddlers' toys litter the lounge. I shall be concentrating, not so much on their inconvenience to me, but rather on how I can help the child's mother to keep the lounge tidy when a clamouring child demands day-long attention. Moreover, when God thus converts our attitudes, he enables us to use our imagination creatively, prompting us, perhaps, to give others pleasant, if mundane surprises: bringing in her washing when it rains; offering to lend him a book you're enjoying; lending her your favourite shampoo; making him a batch of buns unasked; giving him a lift to work.

These generous gestures communicate a healing message: 'It matters to me about you. We may not always see eye to eye about everything, but I care about you as a person, as a member of our household.' Conflict cannot coexist long with this mutual determination to serve.

When we care in this way, the sorrows and frustrations, joys and hopes of members of the household will concern us, though not overburden us. We will not always wait to be *told* how the others are feeling. We will learn to interpret the unspoken messages they communicate. We will make ourselves available to them. We will sense their need and seek to meet it appropriately and with sensitivity. In this way, we will enable others in the household to become familiar with themselves, their fears and frustrations, as well as their joys. In short, we will befriend, seek to understand, receive and accept the others as they really are, not as we would like them to be.

When people in the same house take responsibility for each other in the way I have described, there is a silent bonding, an unspoken agreement, 'We are *for* each other, not against each other.' This commitment does not collapse in the face of conflict. In a mysterious way, conflict strengthens it.

Let there be spaces in your togetherness

A friend of mine who lives in a Christian community seemed embarrassed when he confessed to me recently: 'Since I lived in community I've become really possessive of my room where I can go in and shut the door and be *me*.' This situation is not as lamentable as he made it sound. Human beings need relationships, as we have seen. They also need space. People living in community must safeguard one another's space: their prayer space, their need for solitude, their need sometimes simply 'to be' and not 'to do'. Conflict sometimes erupts because one person's need for this space is greater than others. Homes exist, not to meet one set of needs only, but for mutuality. Therefore we must learn to ask in the face of such conflict, 'Whose needs are greatest today? My need for companionship? Or the other's need for aloneness?' We must learn to be generous at such times in conceding to another's need if it is greatest. Homes are, after all, schools of self-forgetting.

Learn to confront

In all healthy, growing relationships an element of confrontation exists. The challenge that faces us as Christians is to learn to confront others as honestly, gently and Christianly as possible. Humour helps. In our homes and households, as indeed elsewhere, our confronting of others should be self-controlled and compassionate. It should be stripped of the condemnatory, judgemental phrases that are designed to wound rather than upbuild. Our aim in confronting others should not be to spark off conflict but to promote peace. If this aim is to be achieved, the tone of voice, the facial expression, the gesticulations, the words, and the time chosen are all important. I think of Doreen and an occasion when she confronted her husband, Jim.

They had just travelled by car from London to their home in Nottingham. They unpacked, and Doreen asked

Jim to check whether he had switched off the car lights. 'I thought I saw their reflection on the road.' Jim said there was no need to check. He clearly remembered switching the lights off.

The phone rang. While Jim answered it, the door bell rang. It was a neighbour. ''Scuse me. Your car lights're on, missus. You'll have a flat battery in the morning.'

Doreen searched for the car keys, went out and turned off the lights. And I waited for the row.

When Jim came back, Doreen said nothing. We had a meal together, then relaxed. Two hours later, in passing, Doreen turned to Jim, placed her hand on his knee, looked into his face with a smile, giggled and said, 'By the way, darling, the nextdoor neighbour came while you were on the phone.' 'Oh! What did *he* want?' 'He came to say we'd left the lights on the car!' 'Oh no! That must've been my fault. I was *sure* I'd turned them off. I am sorry, darling. I'll go and deal with it straight away.' Doreen laughed. 'It's OK. I've done it.'

This loving, gentle, patient, eye-twinkling confrontation works wonders. Christians creating a home together must similarly learn the art of caring confrontation. The aim of confrontations is not that I demand my pound of flesh but that we are united in Christ.

Confrontation is an essential part of communication. As we have seen, good, clear communication is as essential to communal living as vitamins are to the body. Therefore we must learn both to confront others and to receive confrontation with the humility Doreen's husband demonstrated.

Some Christians make the mistake of tolerating unacceptable behaviour for the sake of a quiet life. This is not the standard of behaviour modelled to us by Jesus. On the contrary, Jesus showed us that confrontation includes rebuking. He once rebuked Peter with these stern words. 'Get thee behind me Satan.' Like Jesus, where necessity demands, we must rebuke others firmly, non-judgementally, without losing our temper or our control.

Confrontation includes challenge. To quote Jesus again: 'Can you drink the cup I must drink?' In other words, 'Can you drink to the dregs the bitter pain-potion I must drink?' 'Couldn't you watch with me one hour?'

Confrontation defines clear boundaries beyond which we will not go. Again, Jesus is our model. He confronted the temple-swindlers with this uncompromising challenge: 'God said, "My Temple will be called a house of prayer. But you have turned it into a hideout of thieves".'

Like Jesus, we must confront but not wound unnecessarily. Much conflict would be eliminated if Christians would confront as Jesus did: with firmness, humour, sensitivity, gentleness and, as we shall emphasize in the last chapter, with the wisdom to choose precisely the correct moment for such communication.

Conflict resolution

What happens in most homes is a heated, speeded-up version of the kind of exchange that took place between Doreen and her husband. One person will whine: 'The neighbour's just been round. You left the lights on the car again. I told you so. Why don't you ever listen?' This provokes a defensive retaliation: 'If you were so cocksure, why didn't you go and switch them off yourself? You've got a set of keys.' The blood of both partners boils. Each attacks the other. They resort to verbal fighting: rudeness, harshness, backbiting, the antitheses of love.

One of the miracles of nature is that snowdrops burst through ice and snow barriers. One of the miracles of home life is that love overcomes hate. We now consider the mystery: how?

Expect to be hurt

Hurting is a part of loving. The more you love someone, the more you expose yourself to being hurt by that person.

Therefore we must expect to be hurt by members of our own household. It is the kind of hurt a widow might experience when the pet cat that has been her constant companion is run over by a car. She finds him in the road, dead, and her sense of loss seems unbearable. Love anyone and you open yourself to being hurt like that. We all know this. Yet when someone we love wounds us, the shock knocks us off-balance and we become like frightened hedgehogs. We curl into a ball, withdraw from others, push out the prickles to protect ourselves and even stab those we love if they come too near too soon. This ball-curling is not necessarily wrong as long as it is temporary. Look at it this way.

Hedgehog prickles are God-made; designed for the hedgehog's preservation. His reflex action, to curl up in a crisis and remain stone still, is natural. Similarly, the hurt and anger we experience when hostility threatens the harmony of the home is a reflex action: neither morally right nor morally wrong.

See hurt and anger as choices to be made

Unless we recognize this, we give Satan a foothold unnecessarily. He will whisper: 'What a weak, pathetic Christian you are. Here you are, pretending to be so Christ-like, yet you're hurt again. You hypocrite.'

Satan delights to condemn. Ignore him. It is not wrong to be hurt by one's friends. Neither is anger, of itself, a sin. If it were, the Bible would not say, 'In your anger do not sin'. It records Jesus' expressed hurt when he stumbled on his sleeping disciples in the Garden of Gethsemane; sleeping when he had begged them for prayer support. This side of eternity we will be angry and hurt. We must view these emotions, not as personal failure, but as a choice to be made. What makes anger and hurt sinful is not the emotional steam they create, what we feel, but how we choose to express those feelings; how we choose to act. If our feet are shod with the Holy Spirit's shoes of peace, we will move through three phases to ensure that conflict strengthens the household and does not destroy it. First, we will heed the clamour of our own emotions.

Listen to your feelings

Listen to the inner anger. Pay attention to the inner hurt. Pour out the full gamut of the feelings to Jesus, the Wonderful Counsellor. I, personally, give vent to such feelings in writing as though God was going to read them. 'Lord, I'm angry this morning. Angry and hurt. I'm angry with myself for expecting Joan to understand how I'm feeling. I'm angry with Joan for the cutting things she said last night. I'm angry because I disobeyed you when you were giving such joy. I'm tired and weary. I could be violent. The other part of me, the hurt part, feels alone. I don't want anyone to see or touch this hurt. I'm tired of being hurt. Tired of forgiving. Please help me.'

God responds to this kind of honest, cleft-stick prayer. He applies healing balm to the hurt places, pours strength into the weariness and replaces distortion with a God perspective that prepares you for phrase two.

Examine yourself objectively

Stage two is this. Ask yourself some searching questions, conscious of the presence of God. 'Why am I angry with X? Because he told me something I needed to hear? Because he was talking rubbish? Because my expectations of him are unrealistic? Because the standard I demand from him is higher than the standard I set for myself? Because I expect him to play the role of God in my life? Because...?' 'What am I going to do about these feelings? Use them to retaliate? Or...?'

Look at the answers to these questions. Refuse to submit to Satan's condemnation: 'You're rotten, useless...'.

Submit instead to the Holy Spirit's conviction: 'Yes. You made a mistake there. God is bigger than your mistakes. Confess. Receive God's forgiveness. Just as God freely forgives you, go on to forgive the person who injured you.'

Forgiveness withheld turns into resentment and bitterness, emotions as invisible but destructive as the dry rot that causes whole buildings to crumble. Forgive, not only the person who harmed you, but yourself also. (Self-belittling is a sin.) Weep over your failure. Bewail your disobedience. But don't wallow in it. The dividing-line between self-pitying remorse and life-giving repentance is finger-nail thin.

Rechannel the energy

There is a third stage in this anger-hurt handling process. Hurt feelings and anger generate energy. This energy, like dynamite, can bring down households, destroy. It can also be as creative as dynamite. Dynamite blasts tunnels through mountains opening up whole new areas for travellers. Similarly, the surge of emotion of hurt or anger can be channelled to remove seemingly insurmountable obstacles. It can also be directed against wrong-doing. Jesus, once more, is our model. At the beginning of his earthly ministry we watch him direct his anger against a prevailing evil: he cleansed the temple from the corrupting influence of money-changers.

'Lord, how can my pent-up feelings be channelled for the good of the household?' This is the prayer that should be born in our heart when we are hurt or angry. Indeed prayer is the key to wholesome households.

Pray

As each individual prays, they plug in, as it were, to the source of pure love, God himself. Thus each person draws from divine love and brings this love back into the mainstream of the home. And I cannot underline enough the importance of whole households praying together. Jesus has promised his presence to the twos and threes who pray together. Shared prayer forces you, among other things, to keep short accounts with one another because you cannot pray together if pressures prise you apart. And in prayer, Jesus is the focus. As you gather round him, like the multi-coloured ribbons children hold when dancing round a may-pole, your lives become intertwined, woven into one another in a kaleidoscope of colour. This intertwining enriches you and adorns the person of Christ.

Conflict, handled in this mature and prayerful way, promotes prolific growth. It draws forth generosity, increases our capacity to forgive, increases our capacity to be hurt (an essential ingredient of love), causes us to re-evaluate our expectations, throws us back on the love of the Lord and prompts us to face up to a life-changing question, 'How are we going to try life another way?'

6
Friction in the Family

Friction in the family is inevitable. At the beginning of Chapter 5, I underlined this uncomfortable fact: friction in the family, or rather lack of it, depends not so much on who you are living with as on who you are. When we submit ourselves to the hand of God that whittles away at our attitudes and behaviour patterns to change and transform them, the atmosphere of our home can radically change. Peggy discovered this when her third child was born.

When Peggy's new baby arrived, the third child under five, she found the days flew by. It seemed one long round of nappy-changing, child-dressing, breast-feeding and child-cajoling. Exhaustion seemed a constant companion, a never-absent shadow.

During the inevitable upheaval to the family routine, Ruth, Peggy's four-year-old, withdrew into her shell. Peggy would often find her just sitting, pale and forlorn, in a corner, sucking her thumb. But Peggy could summon neither the energy nor the resources to play with her lonely little girl and she and Ruth seemed to grow further and further apart. At mealtimes, when Peggy would be holding the baby, feeding her eighteen-month-old and hoping that Ruth, at least, would feed herself, Ruth would clamour for her mummy's attention, whimper, snuggle close to her mother and whine if her food wasn't mashed like her baby brother's. Peggy recognized the signs of need-love, even of sibling rivalry, but her patience and strength were already overstretched. Her resilience was gone. She could not bring herself to take control of the situation. Instead, as the weeks passed by, resentment of Ruth's babyish behaviour took root in Peggy. It spread until it was as rampant and damaging as bindweed in a country garden. When Peggy described the situation to me, she admitted that she nagged Ruth constantly; that Ruth was becoming increasingly withdrawn and insecure.

Resentment, bitterness and intolerance are corrosive sins. They gnaw at a person causing certain death to Christlike love. Peggy recognized this and tipped out the rubble of her rebel emotions at the foot of the cross. As she luxuriated in the forgiveness God freely gave, she repented, that is, she determined to turn back on the past pattern of behaviour; to try to relate to Ruth another way. We prayed that hatred would be dislodged by free-flowing love for Ruth: God's love flowing through her mother to reach Ruth. Little by little, Peggy's attitude changed. She enjoyed meeting Ruth from school, carved out a special 'Ruth-half-hour' before tea, read her stories at night. Ruth's eyes regained her sparkle. She and her mummy had fun together again. The thumb-sucking stopped. More important, the atmosphere in the entire family changed.

While Peggy nagged Ruth, requiring her to change, nothing happened. When Peggy admitted that *she* needed to be changed by God, a quiet miracle took place that benefited the entire family.

Parents, mothers in particular, are the pivot on which the family turns. Whether friction in the family becomes frightening, fragmenting or fortifying depends largely on how parents handle it. In this chapter, then, we focus on family life and examine two questions: Why does friction erupt so frequently? In what way can we call this friction a friend?

Why does friction frequently erupt?

Ask any parents of young children why friction frequently erupts in the family and you will be given ready, takeaway answers. 'I didn't want that screaming scrap of humanity in the first place. She was an accident. The contraceptives let me down, I wanted freedom, not a clamouring child.'

'Friction frequently erupts in our family over discipline. The children don't understand that we really do know what's best for them; that we're not just spoilsports.'

'It's the sheer inconvenience of being tied to the tinies all day. I go to make a phone call. They choose that moment to want me. Have you tried phoning someone or praying with children climbing all over you all the time?'

All of us who are parents know how easy it is to allow the friction that erupts for such reasons to flame into a consuming fire. You take little Johnny to the shops. You are in a hurry. Johnny chooses today to contemplate every daisy and rose bud *en route* to the shops. Your irritation level rises until you snap. Johnny gets a spanking for something trivial. Or your teenager chooses to cover her wall with ghoulish posters. They stare down at you if ever you are allowed into her room to change the sheets or hoover. You wonder how she can sleep under such horrendous pictures. You worry about the influence these pictures have on her. You fear for her future. Will she be able to stand firm as a Christian in a pagan world?

What is going on here in these ordinary, mundane, everyday occurrences? The surface reason for friction is Johnny's snail-like progress to the shopping precinct; the teenager's outlandish chain of choices; conception against all the contraceptive odds. But what are the real reasons for conflict? What are the root causes?

The challenge of parenthood: the demands of selflessness

The underlying reason for friction in the family is the challenge of child-bearing or, more accurately, the challenge of parenthood. Faced with the demands of pregnancy and the helplessness of the newborn baby entrusted to us, we are confronted by the need for supreme self-sacrifice. For a few days or a few weeks, we give of ourselves gladly and generously to the tiny life that sprang from both of us: the fruit of our marital love. But the novelty soon wears off. We are confronted, perhaps more powerfully than ever before, with the truth about ourselves: that we were born with a bias to sin, self-centredness. We want our own way just as badly as our offspring demand that their needs are met. Immediately. The path of self-sacrifice seems irksome. The years spread out before us not as a joyous, romantic adventure but as a dark tunnel through which we must crawl, denying self, maybe even suffering the humility of the self rubbed out. In the face of such selflessness, we squeal.

The challenge of detachment

The second challenge of parenthood is the need for detachment. As a parent, particularly as a mother, you are required to donate all you have and all you are to the little life who has been born or adopted into your family. You deny yourself in order to fulfil the needs of these little ones. But you are not permitted to become over-attached to these young lives. Clench your fists round them with a clinging, smothering, claustrophobic love and you and they are lost. Seek to meet your love-needs through them and you and they will be impoverished. Children are not treasures to be possessed. Children are a trust from God, temporary guests, free people who must be allowed to stay, and, when the time is ripe, to go, to experiment to try life *their* way. Children are not extensions of their parents' personality. They are God-made personalities in their own right. Though they are offshoots of parental love, God created a unique mould for each one. That is why you often hear parents exclaim, 'They're all *our* children but they are all so different.'

The challenge of parenthood, from the toddler stage onwards, is the challenge to succour and yet to let go. The toddler must be given the warmth and security of the parents' love. He must also be given free and fearless space away from parents where he can try life his own way. Unless the toddler takes initiative at this stage and gains autonomy, he will have trouble later on in leaving home and travelling on alone. As parents, we must hold these two child-needs in tension: keep a healthy balance between providing the home-soil where our children can put down roots and where their uniqueness might flourish and at the same time granting them appropriate freedom, the separateness from us where they learn to take initiative. Much of the friction that erupts in the family happens because as parents we wear huge L plates. We are learners, not experts, in parenting. That is why friction is a friend, as we shall go on to observe. It teaches us where we need to adjust our parenting so that it more accurately meets the needs of these little visitors: our children.

The call to trust

At the teenage stage, perhaps the biggest challenge to parents, the one that causes most conflict, is the challenge to trust. Just as your daughter leaves home for university you hear that the tutor in her hall of residence has been offering drugs to undergraduates. Is your daughter strong enough to resist the temptation? You observe the way your teenagers dress: the tight T-shirts, the slinky jeans. Can they resist the pull of the flesh, refrain from living promiscuously? You catch a glimpse of the newspaper headlines: murder, rape—in your area of the city. Dare you allow your sons, let alone your daughters, to step out of your house at night? Your teenager is invited to a party. Midnight strikes and she is still out. Should you go to bed and assume she will come home? Or do you have a parental responsibility to wait up until the key turns in the lock? Your son wants to go camping with his girlfriend. What if...?

Decisions, decisions, decisions. Fear, fear, fear. This is the world of the teenage parent. You have never travelled this way before. How are you supposed to know the answers to these questions that crowd in on you every day? Where does trust end and parental irresponsibility begin? This underlying uncertainty and parental panic is one of the chief causes of conflict at the teenage stage. To love appropriately sometimes demands difficult decisions. It sometimes requires unpopular restrictions. Unless you are secure in yourself and in the Lord, you will find yourself torn in shreds emotionally, an insecurity that will express itself in the nagging syndrome teenagers so dread.

The vocation of parenthood

But the biggest challenge to Christian parents is the challenge to grow in Christlikeness. In fact, it is more fundamental than that because all Christians share that calling. The vocation of parenthood is not simply to house and to clothe, care for and provide for your children, the chief challenge is that you are confronted with a prototype of parenthood, which you are to copy in your behaviour: the fatherhood of God. It is a sobering thought that the first glimmer of God's love which filters through to our children, comes through the vehicle of parental love. Parents who take this responsibility seriously are sometimes filled with a sense of awe, of inferiority or inadequacy. And rightly so. How can we hope to reflect to our children the love that burns in the Father-heart of God for them? Yet this is our calling. During the children's growing years the family must be that place where the parents so pour out Christlike love on their children that, in time, these children will become fellow pilgrims on the journey into life.

Feelings of failure

Friction in the family highlights our failure to reach these goals. This kind of friction generates more friction. I feel a failure because I smacked little Johnny because he dawdled on his way to the shops. Little Johnny was fractious in the supermarket because I was cross with him on the way there. I scold him for whining his way round the supermarket. And so on...By the end of the day the feelings of failure are overwhelming and I am tempted to bewail my lot. 'Lord, why on earth did you entrust me with children?'

Lack of availablility

If you love someone, one expression of that love is to make yourself available to that person. One reason why friction in the family is a common occurrence is that, as parents, we do not model ourselves on this characteristic of the Fatherhood of God. We make ourselves available to our children when it suits us: when the commercials are on, when the news has finished, 'When I've finished the ironing'. Children are quick to detect this reluctant, limited availability. They resent it and rebel.

God offers us unlimited availability. With the heavenly Father we neither need to choose our time carefully nor have an access card to come into his presence. The invitation is unambiguous and clear. 'You may come into my presence with boldness at any time.' This is the availability we should offer to our children.

Of course, I do not mean that we should waive aside the need for discipline, that we should encourage our children to clamour endlessly. What I am suggesting is that we should share the *attitude* that clearly characterizes God: total availability. There is a paradox here. When a child knows that he is welcome at any time, that he can have our undivided attention when he needs it, he clamours less and not more. He is secure in the availability of your love.

Lack of absolute demands

But, of course, this availability is only one of the characteristics of parenthood God-style. Another facet that complements rather than contradicts what we have already said is that our heavenly Father makes absolute demands on his children and expects unwavering obedience; even when he requires his first-born to stagger under Calvary's cross. One reason why friction spoils family life these days is that many parents do not operate within this biblical framework. They are afraid to discipline, afraid to set clear goals for their children, afraid to demand absolute obedience. Where there is little obedience there is little trust. Where there is little trust there is little love. Where there is little love there is much friction. Friction arises because of the insecurity lack of discipline brings. Love for children will express itself in nurturing them with self-sacrificing availability but will also provide plenty of information and clear instructions about the 'how to' of negotiating the uphill struggle of life. Children may resist these demands. They may call parents 'square', 'fuddy-duddy', 'mean'. But eventually they will understand, love them and maybe even thank their parents. It happened to a friend of mine unexpectedly.

She was talking to another friend, Pauline, about her rebellious teenager. Her own daughter, also a teenager, was there. Pauline expressed her alarm, 'Jan wants to spend over £20 on a pair of shoes.' 'Are you going to give in?' To this question, Pauline admitted, 'I'll have to. There'll be such a rumpus if I don't. Anything for a quiet life.'

When my friend left that house, her daughter reminded her of a similar tussle they had had a few weeks earlier. My friend had set limits on the amount her daughter could spend on shoes. 'Am I being stingy?' she had asked herself at the time. Now, her daughter admitted: 'I'm glad you didn't allow me to spend as much as I liked. I was really pushing you to see how far you'd let me go. I need your guidance, your wisdom and your help.'

God, in his love and mercy, never kowtows to inappropriate needs. Rather, he offers clear guidelines and says, 'This is the way. Walk here.' He expects our obedience. If we are to reflect God's love to our children we must do the same. To offer them less will not lead to frictionlessness. It might earn us peace and quiet for a while. Eventually it will result in parent-belittling. Children need to know their parents are in control.

Lack of time and affirmation

Time is one of the most precious gifts we have to give to our children. Much of the conflict that creates heartaches in families today arises because parents deny their children the offer of this priceless gift.

It is easier to give your children an expensive toy than to play with him, but most children prefer cardboard, crayons, scissors and Mother's or Father's undivided attention to costly toys. Expensive toys are often nine-day wonders. If they are not broken first, they lie, unused, in the toy cupboard unless Mum or Dad plays with them too. Donate your leisure time to your children. Explore life together so that they are exposed to stimulating experiences. Broaden their horizons, but do it with them. Swim with them. Walk with them. Watch television with them. Much of the whining that triggers off quarrels will stop when our children are assured that we love them enough to give them our time.

Similarly, all children need the affirmation of their parents. Children are growing up in an increasingly competitive world. Little girls of three or four compete for a place advertising soap on the commercials. Toddlers compete at playschool. Teenagers compete for a job or a place at college or university. A certain amount of competition is healthy; adds zest to life. But all competition and no affirmation results in inner loneliness and insecurity. God, our heavenly parent-figure, frequently affirms his children. 'You are my friends.' 'I have told you everything.' 'Well done, good and faithful servant.' 'I haven't met such faith in Israel.' Similarly, we must affirm our children. When the toddler walks, uses new words, learns to use the potty for himself, praise him. Build up his self-esteem. This will not turn him into the dreaded spoilt child. It will give him the certainty that he is lovable, capable, of worth. It will spur him on to more achievements.

The same applies in the teen-scene. Teenagers may behave in a brash, insensitive way. This is often a mask camouflaging insecurities and uncertainties. It is easy, especially at this stage, to recognize the behaviour that irritates us as parents, to believe that we have a duty to point out weaknesses. In doing so, we often magnify the failure that already plagues the teenager concerned and thereby spark off friction. What our son or daughter longs for and would respond to is not criticism, but affirmation and affection. Reflect back to them all that is of worth in them. They may have lost touch with this part of themselves. It will encourage them to press on towards personal growth. It will also increase their respect for you. Life will not be friction-free. As we have already seen, a certain amount of friction is inevitable in family life. But where the pervading atmosphere is affirmative and affectionate love, friction can set you free; free to try life in a new way, free to grow. At least, whenever I rub up against my heavenly Father, such is the level of affirmation and affection welling up in his Father-heart, that this friction frees me for further growth. Friction becomes not an ogre but a friend.

Lack of acceptance

One of the amazing facets of divine love is that it is accepting love. God sees me just as I am, 'warts n'all', and loves me just as I am. The lack of this qualitative, accepting love in families fans friction into flames. An eleven-year-old sums up the situation well in a poem called *Me*:

> If anyone's in trouble,
> it's Me!
> If the cat gets no milk,
> it's Me!
> If a knife drops, or a door bangs,
> it's Me!
> Me! Me! Me!
> it's always Me!...
> If the baby start screaming,
> it's Me!
> If the fuse is broken,
> it's Me!
> Me! Me! Me!
> It's always (guess who!)
> ME!
> (Susan Stowe (age eleven), *Fresh Voices*, NCER, 1979 para. 59.)

When a child is bombarded with continuous criticism, when parents fall into the trap of viewing their children as flesh-and-blood Pinocchios, puppets to be controlled rather than children to be loved, when parents offer love in exchange for good behaviour, the scene is set, not just for friction in the family, but for something far more serious: the smouldering resentment that becomes the seed-bed for doubts about personal self-worth and lovability. God never measures out this cruel treatment. Instead he offers us acceptance in such large doses that we, ourselves, desire to change as a response of love to Love.

Lack of forgiveness

And, if we are to model our parenting on the Fatherhood of God, forgiveness will always be near at hand.

Friction in the family can produce prolific growth, as we shall go on to observe. It can also become like smouldering embers in the grate, ready to be fanned into flames unless certain procedures are observed.

As parents we must be ever ready to forgive member(s) of the family who caused the friction. We must think more of their welfare and the well-being of the family than ourselves. We must safeguard their wholeness, confronting if necessary, but continuing to love. This love, though sorely bruised, can break the chain of conflict. It can prevent resentment and retaliation perpetuating family friction. The extrovert parent will find this much easier than the reflective, introverted type. But it must be done. As Christians we are not permitted to focus on friction for ever. Outrageous behaviour can be dealt with in one of two ways: with punishment or with forgiveness. God's way is to forgive. God commands us to forgive. Forgiveness breaks through the vicious circle of attack and counter-attack, accusation and retaliation. Forgiveness is the hand of faith that holds the friction-filled family into the reconciling, healing love of God, believing that his love can hold the family together. Forgiveness is not the same as forgetting. When you forgive you may remember the full extent of the pain inflicted yet you can look the person in the eye and tell them that they are forgiven, loved, valued. Such forgiving releases others from the bondage of hatred in which we have trapped them.

Lack of prayer

You cannot pray with someone against whom you hold a grudge. Perhaps that is why the old cliché claims, 'The family which prays together stays together'. Charlie Shedd, an American marriage counsellor, underlines the value of shared prayer with the remarkable observation that he has never counselled a Christian couple who pray together regularly. He has counselled a few who said they used to.

Lack of shared prayer as a family undoubtedly gives rise to much unnecessary friction. Don't allow family prayers to become a burden. Let them be a delight: the whole family sitting on Tim's bedroom rug, praying together before he goes to bed; the whole family praying together in the car before they set off on holiday; the family listening to worship choruses at lunchtime. When our family were young, we kept family prayers for special days, like our weekly day off. Praying together as a complete family was a treat we looked forward to, not a burden imposed in the rush and tumble of getting ready for school. Or I think of the family we stayed with in Poland. Mealtimes are leisurely, together-times. Before the meal, the family pray together: short, simple, sincere prayers.

We have highlighted some of the characteristics of the Fatherhood of God. I recognize that this list could be daunting for some parents, even guilt-inducing. My aim in calling to mind the divine prototype is not to rub your nose in failure but rather to provide some reasons why family life sometimes seems so full of friction. Where fathers and mothers fall short of God's standards for parents, opportunities for friction come flooding in. But even if parents were perfect, friction would still erupt because we parents have given birth to babies with a strong bias to disobedience. Jesus' relationships with his family were far from friction-free, even though he *was* perfect. It seems, then, that we are saddled with conflict so we might as well learn to use it constructively, to refuse it permission to destroy family life. Our next task is to discover how to work conflict into our lives so that, like yeast acting on dough or ginger on beef in Chinese cooking, it affects the whole of family life for good. The more I do this, the more firmly I conclude that friction is nothing more, nor less, than homework to be done:

thoroughly, systematically and well.

Friction: homework to be done

I make this claim because I am learning that, when friction frightens me, threatening to disrupt the family, the fellowship or friendships, there are five questions I must face. First, 'What new insights can I glean from this situation: about myself, my family, life, God?' Second, I must take full responsibility for my share in the blame and ask, 'What mistakes have *I* made?' Third, 'What is going on underneath the surface, causing this conflict to erupt?' Fourth, 'Is the underlying cause pain and sadness in the person with whom I am cross. Do they need compassion rather than my annoyance?' Fifth, 'What is God trying to teach me through this frightening situation?'

Peggy, whom I mentioned at the beginning of this chapter, worked through these questions faithfully. As she did so, she discovered that friction with Ruth was a friend in disguise. Friction with her daughter Ruth was the faithful friend that wounded her so that, eventually, she cried out for healing and in turn became an instrument of God's healing and love to her little girl.

If we allow it to be, friction can always befriend in this way. When friction flies round family life like a bluebottle in summer, ask yourself some forthright questions. Is this highlighting slip-shod parenting? Am I modelling myself on the Fatherhood of God or has worldliness crept into our family philosophy? What is God trying to say to me through this situation? How is he trying to bring me into alignment with his will? Is he asking me to grow in certain areas: the ability to trust, the selflessness that places parenthood above profession or pride, the guts to give guidance?

If friction in the family highlights failure in yourself, don't wallow in remorse or self-pity. Confess. Enjoy the forgiveness God gives. Determine to try life another way, reflecting more accurately the love of the Father to his children. And don't grumble, an art in which most Christians excel. Rather, seek grace to grow: to grow in maturity and wisdom, in discernment and generous love, in Christlike compassion and care. If friction goads you into such growth in the same way as it has gradually changed many parents before you, then friction in the family will not simply have been work to be done, a challenge to be confronted, it will indeed have become a faithful friend: the one who wounds to heal, the one who pressurizes, not to break down, but to restore. No family will ever be fully free of friction. But by God's grace, many families can discover that friction propels people into ever-increasing freedom.

7

When Love Threatens to Collapse

The dividing line between love and hate is gossamer thin. I rediscovered this for myself as I was about to begin this chapter. My husband and I had enjoyed a day out together: browsing in the market of a country town near our home, tramping in the hills under a steel-blue autumn sky, going out together for the evening on our own, a rare treat.

When we arrived home, I went to the kitchen to make the bedtime drinks. David wandered off to watch the news on television. And something inside me snapped. I felt irritated, annoyed abandoned. It may be irrational, but I wanted him to be with me. It had been such a good day, why stay apart now? When he went off like that, I felt rejected. Of course I hadn't actually *said*, 'Let's make the drinks together.' Neither had he said, 'Do you mind if I watch the news?' But the hurt inflicted resulted in me rediscovering the horrifying truth that hatred can displace love as quickly as you can snap open an automatic umbrella. The reason for this, of course, is that hatred is love hurt.

We have already noted in this book that the risk you take when you love someone is that you will be hurt. Indeed the more you love someone the more you open yourself to being hurt by that person. It is all very well to store up these well-known facts in the retrieval system of our minds, but there are certain other facts with which we should acquaint ourselves. Unless we do so, conflict could become a catastrophe instead of a piece of constructive work to be done.

The personal illustration I have described was painful but trivial. It was cleared up in five minutes when David and I talked about it a few minutes later. But the love-hate syndrome is not always relieved so swiftly. Indeed, for many people love has collapsed altogether. I think of the vicar's wife who once telephoned me. She told me that her husband didn't love her any more, that he had found a younger woman who understood and sympathized with him, that he wanted his wife and children out of the home by Christmas so that his girlfriend could move in. Or I think of the young man who wrote to me recently telling me that his fiancée had broken off their engagement: 'She seems to want her freedom more than she wants me.' And I recall the thirty-year-old who introduced herself to me a few weeks ago, an attractive young mother with two delightful children. 'I'm trying to adjust to a new lifestyle now that we're a one-parent family.'

Splintering marriages, broken engagements, family breakdown are common phenomena today. They add up to a great deal of heartache and heartbreak. It is to this heartbreak situation that I hope to speak in this chapter, asking four basic questions. What happens inside a person when their partner doesn't love them any longer? How does this affect their behaviour? How should we handle the powerful emotions that surge to the surface when love is threatened? How can the inner conflict that arises be used constructively?

When love is withdrawn: anxiety

One of the first things that happens when a loving relationship is threatened by one partner withdrawing their commitment is that the abandoned partner experiences deep anxiety. The young man whose fiancée broke off the engagement wrote: 'I love her. How will I live without her? Is there any way I can persaude her to stay with me?' The wife whose husband told her he didn't love her any longer wept down the phone: 'I'm sure it's not right that we should part. But how can I keep him? Is there anyone we can talk to...anything we can do?' The young man who lives with the dread that his girlfriend no longer loves him, threatens to commit suicide, his way of blackmailing her to marry him. The anxious partner spends time and energy pleading and cajoling, crying and threatening. Sometimes this results in dramatic scenes, angry outbursts, accusations followed by counter-accusations. The longer the threat of separation hovers over the household, the higher the level of anxiety will rise. This anxiety may express itself in sleeplessness, frequent quarrels, an accumulation of bitterness, irritability. If the children misbehave, their disobedience is met by a snappy response or the punishment administered is far more severe than the behaviour warrants. In other words, the anxiety level has risen so dangerously high that, like a river about to burst its banks, the welter of accumulated feelings overflow at the slightest provocation. Conflict, with all its power to destroy, surges downstream persistently and relentlessly.

Abandonment

One of the reasons for this uncontrollable anxiety is that the person whose loved one threatens to leave is gripped by the pain of abandonment, a pain that equals the distress a child experiences when it is left with or without explanation by his parents. Just as the child protests, screams, kicks, yells, throws a tantrum and then quietly withdraws into a silent shell if his parents fail to return, so the adult protests, despairs or nosedives into depression if he is threatened with the loss attached to abandonment. The protesting may be expressed by shouting, crying, screaming, blaming, accusing or threatening behaviour. The adult might turn to

drink, like the young wife who told me, 'When I discovered
he's been having an affair with another woman, I put up a
camp bed in the lounge, bought myself a bottle of wine and
drank it until I couldn't feel the pain any more.' Or the
abandoned partner might even try to end it all. 'When my
husband didn't come back, I reached for the aspirin bottle
and swallowed fifteen. Mercifully, I was sick an hour or so
later.' Quite often, the threat of the loss of the loved one is
enough to push the rejected partner into the depths of
darkness and depression.

Loss

A person accustomed to the undivided love of the partner
who has now ceased to care suffers an intolerable loss.
There is the loss of self-esteem, the loss of the one-to-one
caring that communicates that you are special to the other,
the loss of security. The abandoned person not only fears
loss, he also feels lost. He does not know who he can trust
any longer, he is directionless, the future looms large,
bleak, frightening and empty.

At first, when the bond of marriage, engagement or
in-loveness is threatened and seems likely to snap, the
partners may quarrel. The conflict dividing them will be
expressed in hurtful and angry encounters. But gradually
this will change. As the hurt goes deeper the couple recoil
from one another. As the gulf between them widens, the
rare exchanges between them will become cool and indif-
ferent. They might then become mildly friendly again. As
one man put it when he described his encounter with his
wife in the divorce court, 'We smiled at each other, even
kissed each other goodbye—just like old friends.'

Defensive detachment

When cool indifference characterizes the communication
that takes place between two people who once enjoyed

intimacy, this is simply the surface expression of a deeper, more significant, response. Just as, in childhood, when the psychological needs of the child are not met by the parent, deep damage takes place in the relationship, so, in adulthood, when persons who once loved each other separate, a serious severance takes place. The abandoned partner, like the hurt child, not only ceases to desire the attachment he once enjoyed, he goes further: he deliberately detaches himself from the former partner to defend himself from further hurt. It is as though these two people were once steam-engines hitched together as they chugged through life. Now they are unhooked. As they go their separate ways the gulf grows ever-wider.

Persons experiencing this ever-widening gulf often express the inner panic with hardness, aloofness, indifference. This might camouflage pain and panic, bitterness and loneliness. Such loneliness frequently leads to hostile behaviour, but the lonely person refuses to be helped. Having loved and been hurt once, they determine to barricade their pain in. That way, perhaps, the pain will go away. At least it can be pushed down, hidden, tucked out of sight.

Mourning

For a person who is thus withdrawing from the former source of love, refusing to trust others, fearing even to depend on God, a process of mourning takes place that is as profound and necessary as the mourning experienced when a loved one is lost through death. If a person in mourning seems shell-shocked, numb, indecisive or irritable, we make allowances for this behaviour. When they express anger, pain, bewilderment or guilt, we know that these are the stepping-stones to the final goodbye of bereavement, that bitter-sweet phase of life when we can wave a fond farewell to what has been and what might have been; when, too, we can turn round and hold out our arms to the future, and to the God who holds the future trusting that, though everyone else may have abandoned us, whatever comes next comes to us with God. God holds our questions and our answers; God has promised always to be there.

Expressing the hurt: irritability

One of the reasons why I have emphasized that love severed frequently results in anxiety, abandonment, depression, loneliness, or mourning is this: when such emotions take us by storm, the little boat of our life receives a severe battering. Most of our energy is spent on negotiating the storm. There is little left for other relationships. Such people often become short-tempered, their nerves are frayed at the edges, they seem brittle, always exhausted. The hate that wells up inside them spills over in inappropriate places and unfortunate ways. The baby is sick down her clean dress. Her fraught mother shakes her, even feels like battering her. Little Mary fails to get to the potty in time. Her mother gives her a vicious spanking before mopping up the puddle on the carpet. The teenagers are nagged: for the clothes they choose and the records they play, for their untidiness and their rudeness. Nothing is right. I am not suggesting that this behaviour is appropriate for the Christian. I am saying that it is understandable; that it explains why some conflict erupts. It is the overspill of grazed emotions: a cry for help.

Anger

A wife whose husband confesses that he has been having an affair with another woman is a wounded woman. A man whose wife tells him that she has become emotionally entangled with another man suffers a severe and injurious shock. The reflex reaction to such news may be an angry response. 'I feel angry with myself. I should have seen it coming. I should have prevented it. I should have been a better husband and then she wouldn't have had to reach out to others for what I failed to give.' 'How can he do this to me and the children after all these years together?'

This anger, of itself, is not morally wrong. It is morally neutral. As we have observed, whether this becomes unrighteous anger or not depends on how it is channelled.

When anger boils over into irritability, bad temper, short-fused angry outbursts or partner-fighting, then it becomes a sin. The sin of uncontrolled and uncontrollable anger in such circumstances is a common one. 'When he told me about the girl he's been sleeping with, I said to him, "How can you witness to others about the Lord when all the while you're doing things like that? You're a hypocrite. You've got to repent. What kind of a father d'you think you are to our children? Look at you now. You sit around here all day expecting me to cook and clean for you when all the while you're wanting to be with that girl..."'

Sarcasm, fault-finding, accusing, refusing to see any good in the partner, backbiting, attacking the *person*, rather than confronting the problem. These are all expressions of the hatred that is conceived in hurt. They are understandable, but inappropriate. Such dirty fighting should be avoided even when you are smarting inside because your partner has wronged you. Such retaliation is not one of the weapons the Holy Spirit permits Christians to use.

The silent treatment

And giving your partner the silent treatment, withdrawing into aloof and ice-cold silence, is equally un-Christlike. Yet the cold war is not uncommon among Christians. 'My wife didn't speak to me for a week after I'd told her our marriage was finished.' Some Christians resort to this kind of behaviour because they believe it is more acceptable than having a row. It isn't. It can be just as damaging, sometimes even more so. It is just as much an expression of conflict as a blazing row.

Stress

When love collapses between partners, both suffer from
intolerable stress. This stress factor cannot be avoided. But
neither hotted-up fight tactics nor flights into frozenness
are adequate methods of expressing the whole gamut of
emotions that surface at a time like this. But the troubled
emotions—guilt, the desire to retaliate, anger, hatred,
wrath—must be dealt with if they are not to lie on the shore
of our lives, as lethal as nuclear-contaminated debris.

How to handle negative emotions

Anger is mentioned many times in the Bible. 'Then the
Lord's anger burned against Moses' (Ex 4:14), 'the fierce
anger of the Lord has not turned away from us' (Jer 4:8),
'He [Jesus] looked round at them in anger' (Mk 3:5). God's
anger is always just, pure, holy. Anger, in man, is a reflex
action, a surge of emotion prompted by certain circumstances. It is biochemical in nature. The reaction *of itself* is
not sin-stained.

As we have seen, what determines whether the reaction
becomes a sin or a sharp sword in the Master's hand is what
we choose to do with it. The problem is that when anger
rises within us like milk coming to the boil, it spills over
before we can reach out to switch off the gas. The choice we
make about what to do with our anger must be made in
split-second timing. That is why anger often turns to sin.
That is why many Christians fail far more through their
reactions than through their carefully planned actions.

When we feel anger coming to the boil inside us, we must
recognize that this is normal, natural, a part of being human.
But we must also acknowledge to ourselves two more truths:
that this anger need not spill over as sin; that if we are
seeking to live biblically and to love others, it *must* not
result in sin. If this is the case, what do we do with such
powerful negative emotions?

Take them to God

The only safe place for hostile feelings—anger, guilt, hatred, the desire for revenge, the longing to retaliate, bitterness—is the cross of Christ. And the only place where healing flows into the hurts that underlie much of this hostility is the lap of God. This is the most appropriate tip for our emotional rubbish.

Some therapists encourage the full expression of negative feelings. 'Pound a pillow, throw crockery against the wall, smash up some old furniture, get the anger out,' they advise. For some people this vicarious ventilation of anger seems to help. What the Christian must not do is to take the next seemingly logical step: to give the offending person a 'piece of your mind', to tear strips off another while the angry feelings are still red-hot. Neither must the offending person's reputation be ruined through gossip and half-truths, responses to anger that occur all too often even in Christian circles. Far too many people have already been ground to powder by such inappropriate expressions of anger. We are to be angry, but not to sin (Eph 4).

When anger rages inside me like a caged animal, I try to go quickly to the cross and ventilate it there. Sometimes it is enough to express my anger verbally. On other occasions such is the strength of the violence, that it seems as though I hammer home the nails that pinned the Lord's body to the tree. On such occasions I am reminded that Jesus can take the full force of my wrath, that he understands, that he hung there for this purpose, to take away my sin. I know, too, that he will receive the mangled mess of my emotions, sift them, keep anything that is worth keeping—the shreds of love—and with the breath of compassion, throw the rest away.

Make them a matter for prayer

The procedure I have described above is a form of praying. There are times when anger stings rather than boils over.

Again, the repository for this anger is the cross of Christ.
See him hanging there, for you. Hand him the bundle. Ask
him to sift it and only to hand back to you anger purified.
The procedure is miracle-working. The sting of the anger is
removed. Hostility evaporates. So much conflict between
Christian couples could be avoided if they would act in this
way rather than reacting in a worldly way: nursing their
anger so that, like a well-fed baby, it grows.

Share your need with another

You may do all this but your circumstances may not change
and the hatred may come back like a flood. Anger might
plunge you into pain. The place for this pain is the lap of
God. Tell him about the hurt. Ask him to heal it. It is often
helpful to talk to someone about the pain, to confess the
hatred and the anger, so that you are not in the hole alone.

Look for someone who will both understand you and
confront you: 'It must be very hard for you at the moment
but have you thought of...'; someone who will face you
with the need to forgive, someone who will hold before you
a biblical standard: the need to resolve conflict, to settle
disputes quickly, the need to refuse to let anger out indis-
criminately, the need to refrain from the uncontrolled
expression of anger that damages others (see Prov 16:32;
Jas 1:19). Avoid the trap of looking for someone who will
simply say what you want them to say.

Refuse to repress your anger

Just as battering others with angry words can bruise them,
so the repression of anger is damaging to ourselves and our
relationships. A friend of mine put it well the other day.
'My pattern of anger is this. I withdraw from my husband
without warning. I become cold, unco-operative, uncom-
municative. He hasn't a clue what is going on and therefore
becomes insecure. Eventually he starts to blame himself.
It's usually at that stage that I emerge from cold storage.'

She emerges from cold storage but her emotions do not.

This woman has learned how to cram her feelings in an already over-full deep freeze. There they hide, frozen, but not dead. They spring to life as anxiety, tension, fatigue, and a variety of physical disorders. They plague the person who sought to stack them away. Their persecution is without mercy.

Forgive

The antidote to repression is forgiveness. Repression is taking all the hostilities, pushing them as far down into the subconscious as possible, and living as though they were not there. Forgiveness is confronting the hostile emotions, owning them as part of our hurting, helpless self, acknowledging who it was who inflicted the injury, and forgiving the offender; setting him free.

To forgive is hard. It was not easy for Jesus to forgive me, to forgive you. It cost him the agony of Gethsemane, the terror of the trial, the humiliation of Golgotha. But he did it. He triumphed. And so must we, no matter how much it costs us, no matter what people do to us. If you cannot forgive, go one step further back in your prayer. Ask God to pour his Spirit of love into your heart—the love that wants to let go of hatred.

When we have forgiven the person who caused the hurting, when we have forgiven those involved in causing the collapse of love, then we are ready to move out of the hurt and abandonment to live life without the loved one, stripped of all that might have been, but held within the all-supporting hand of God.

Learning from conflict: about yourself

This stage will not be reached without a struggle and much pain but many lessons will have been learned along the way. Such conflict is a teacher who presents us with home-work to be done. For example, 'Respond to these questions: What has this collapse of love taught me about myself?

What is it teaching me about the Christian life? What can I learn about relationships? What am I discovering about the Lord? What am I learning about life?' A friend of mine whose marriage broke down several years ago now looks back and sees how God used conflict to draw her to himself, to increase her sensitivity to the needs of others, to help her mature. If we will learn, conflict will teach.

Conflict also teaches us about ourselves as Louise discovered after her engagement broke up. 'It really taught me that I'm desperate to get married. That's the real pain I must hold into the Lord's hands.' As Louise worked through the hurt, conflict made a profound contribution to her growth in Christ. She learned not to hammer to God when life hurts, but instead to trust him with the real situation, the pain that paralyses. 'Lord, I'm hurting because I'm alone. Please come to me.' God answers prayers like that.

In an attempt to keep her fiancé, Louise had capitulated to his demands and slept with him. The quarrels that erupted because of this taught her another unforgettable lesson: joy in Christ and disobedience do not mix. It is when you repent and turn back to God that joy also returns.

Learning from conflict: about priorities

Mandy and Chris also reminisce, somewhat ruefully, about their experience of love lost. 'Chris used to be away from Monday to Friday every week. He would live in one hotel after another because of his job. It was all right while he was away. I coped. But when he came back on Friday nights it was a different story. He would want to stay at home all weekend. He'd been out enough. But I was longing for a change of scenery. He wanted simple home cooking after hotel food all week. But I was longing to be taken out for a meal after cooking all week. Our lives were almost incompatible. We learned from that to plan our priorities differently. It was the only way of saving our marriage.'

Learning from conflict: about detachment

Many marriages are not saved. Sylvia looks back, not only on a disastrous marriage but on those traumatic years when her children reached the turbulent teens. 'I didn't know how to be mother *and* father to my two. I overprotected my teenage daughter; smothered my son so that he became a mummy's boy. No wonder they both left home at the earliest possible opportunity. I hated them going, though. I suppose it showed me what I was doing—seeking to have all my love-needs met through my children. It took me a long time to discover that's not what children are for. I'm still learning to live a meaningful life without them. Through all the rows and riots we endured, God taught me a certain amount of detachment.'

God took Chris and Mandy through the hard school of conflict and taught them the vital art of re-examining their priorities from time to time. He also met Sylvia in that same school and taught her the even more difficult skill of detachment, the letting go even of those we love for their good and God's glory. This stripping of self and denial of one's own needs is often most thoroughly learned as a result of the fight we put up to hold on to those we thought were our possessions when, after all, they were only on trust from God.

Learning from conflict: about God

Betsy ten Boom used to say in Ravensbruck, 'No pit is too deep but God is deeper still.' It is in this pit of despair and disillusionment, fear and heartache, that God reveals himself as God-with-us, God born into the abyss of human abandonment and pain. It is there that he meets us and we know ourselves held, understood and met by him. We find ourselves coping with crises, not in our own puny strength, but with his. We cope with the bereavement love lost inevitably inflicts. We cope with the need to unclench our fists and let go of certain loves. We open our hands and receive healing, new trust, new love. We amaze ourselves as we discover the resilience to live life a new way. We discover that this process is not painless but it is possible. It is possible because, co-operating with him, all things are possible.

Learning from conflict: about helping

In time, we may find that the lessons we learned through conflict have an even deeper purpose under God. I think of Maisie. Her marriage, less than a year old, is disintegrating fast. I can hold out a helping hand, but I cannot feel the full extent of her pain because I have never stood in that frightening place. 'Do you know anyone who's been through this and survived?' Maisie asked. I was able to say that I did; able to link her up with Linda. Linda's marriage collapsed like a pack of cards a few years ago. Because Linda learned not to hate, but to so forgive that she could go on living and to go on loving, she is now in a position to rescue others from the foaming sea of emotions that threaten life itself when love dies. It is Linda who rescued Maisie because conflict so refined her life that she is God-equipped to help others.

8

Friction in the First Phase of Marriage

For many couples, the first year of marriage is the worst. The first phase of marriage, the first two or three years, are make-or-break years. During this period, the foundations of the marriage are laid, habits and behaviour patterns that set the pace for the future marriage are formed and the couple succeed or fail in becoming 'primary resource persons' to one another, that is, the most significant person in their partner's life. If firm, stable foundations are laid the marriage and future family has got off to a good start; life-patterns established in these early days are not easily changed. If the couple learn to adapt to one another in generous, mutually supportive ways, it augurs well for the future. If the couple so learn to adapt to each other that each finds their primary place of belonging to one another, then the marriage is not only firm and steady but life-giving also.

But few couples get it right at once. That is why the first few years of marriage are often full of frustrations and friction. This friction can be a friend or it can become a deadly foe.

Many couples view friction in the first few years as an ogre, the spoilsport who mars the romantic, euphoric relationship enjoyed by the couple in the engagement and post-honeymoon months, the enemy who plots and succeeds in bringing their once-idyllic relationship to an abrupt and sticky end. I think of one girl I know who was married at eighteen and divorced before she was twenty. Or of another, who was married in her second year at university and divorced before she had graduated. Or of yet another, a young woman whose marriage of eleven months is already in a serious state of disrepair, whose husband is pushing her to seek for a divorce.

The heartbreak situations are not rare. It is now generally accepted that the first five years of marriage form one of the peak periods of marital breakdown in the West today. Statistics show that in the last few years, the divorce rate among the under twenty-five-year-olds has *trebled*. In one survey it was discovered that, among the divorced population, half of the marital problems that eventually resulted in the break-up of the marriage, had emerged by the second wedding anniversary, and 37% of those divorced had separated by their fifth wedding anniversary. These statistics are the crust covering unimaginable, indescribable heartache for countless men, women and children. It is a serious problem to which we must apply ourselves in this chapter.

I propose to do two things. First, to explain some of the reasons why frustation in the first five years is a frequent occurrence. Second, to show how this friction can become a friend and not a foe.

Fragile—handle with care

An infant marriage, like a young seedling, is fragile. It needs to be handled with care, protected and nurtured so that it may put down roots, send out shoots, and grow strong and fruitful.

One of the reasons why the young marriage is fragile is that both partners forming the marriage are in a state of transition. It is quite possible that the bride will have been transplanted from one part of the country to another.

I think of Karen. She is young, vivacious, highly qualified.

Her relationship with her parents is good, happy and supportive. When she was single she was never short of friends. Recently she married. She moved to a large city in the Midlands where unemployment is high. When she returned from her honeymoon reality hit her. She and her husband were enjoying making his bachelor-pad into a home, but what of the future? In this vast concrete jungle she was friendless, jobless, and far away from her family. When she married, she gained a husband whom she loved passionately, but this gain was counterbalanced by a series of losses: loss of status, loss of independence, and worse, loss of certain securities on which she had learned to rely. Of course, the bliss of the post-honeymoon period compensated for many of these losses, but when Karen searched the small ads every lunchtime and every evening hoping for a job where her qualifications could be put to good use, she would also become aware of uncomfortable uncertainties vying for her attention. 'Who am I?' 'Where do I belong?' As the months wore on, she admitted to herself that, though married, she was lonely.

No one had warned Karen that it could be like this. No one had even so much as hinted that for many brides, waves of loneliness can sweep over them like waves battering the cliffs that frame the seashore. So Karen felt cheated: cheated by God, cheated by marriage, cheated by her husband.

Her husband. Wasn't he supposed to meet all her needs now that they were married? When he came home in the evening, he would sometimes discover, not the sweet, loving wife who doted on him, but an irritable, snappy, bad-tempered young woman who would bite his head off if he slurped his tea, nag if he left his pyjamas in a heap on the bedroom floor as he'd always done when he was single, and fly off the handle at the slightest provocation.

These situations are not rare. Although few couples confess that this kind of conflict exists in the early months of marriage, they are common as couples come to terms with the adjustments required of this first phase of life together.

They are brought to the surface by loneliness, loss and displacement.

Loss

When Karen let go of singlehood, she lost its freedom, her independence and self-fulfilment. She has exchanged these for a set of new losses: loss of job, loss of friends, loss of familiarity, loss of the place of belonging. For some people, loss equals challenge. They make the necessary adjustments with ease, even with verve. But for others, such displacement, even by that which is good, is alarming until they have re-established a new rhythm, established a routine, and identified a place to belong. Those for whom displacement is painful, who feel the losses more acutely than the compensatory gains, find the early days of marriage difficult, even lonely. They must be understood, loved and gentled along.

Loneliness

It is unfashionable for newly-weds to admit that they sometimes suffer pangs of loneliness. Only in the counselling room, it seems, are couples honest enough to admit, 'I am more lonely now I'm married than when I was single.'

But such loneliness is not rare. From its pain springs much of the friction that causes young marriages to fly apart. A wife is lonely so she blames her husband for not meeting all her love-needs. A husband misses his former friends and is lonely without their companionship. He nags his wife to invite them round for meals and fails to recognize that this round of cooking, cleaning and entertaining is siphoning off energy she needs to make the emotional adjustments of early marriage. Thus friction becomes a foe: the dynamite that blows the couple apart. As we shall go on to see later in this chapter, this situation need not end in calamity. It can result in prolific growth.

Number one

Of course, some adjustments are fun. Decorating your home is fun, furnishing the home is fun, finding homes for the wedding presents is fun. But even this fun can be fraught with friction.

'We began to decorate our flat. I wanted a blue bedroom and brown kitchen. But he doesn't like blue and he doesn't like brown. All my cherished plans had to be discarded.'

'We were trying to decide how to furnish our home. We'd decided on a bedroom suite as a must. We could make do elsewhere but we wanted our bedroom to be really nice. Then his auntie threw a spanner in the works. She wanted to give us an old chest of drawers. It was a beautiful piece of furniture, I must admit, probably an antique. She'd have *given* it to us, too. My husband wanted it. I didn't. The resentment this old chest of drawers caused between us smouldered for weeks. Eventually we said "No" but I still feel guilty about it.'

Concrete things like furniture and colours are not the only pressure points, unfortunately. More serious incompatibilities disrupt the relationship as time creeps on. 'My wife drives me mad at bedtime. We go up to the bedroom together. I jump into bed, ready for a cuddle and sleep. I don't know what she finds to do but she fiddles around for hours before eventually climbing into bed. Then she complains because I fall asleep as soon as my head hits the pillow.'

'It's the little things that throw us. He's so fussy about tidiness; always grumbling if he finds crumbs on the carpet or a thin layer of dust on the furniture. But I'm busy. Life is bigger than hoovering and dusting in my view. Who's right?'

Sleeping patterns, eating patterns, attitudes, priorities: these all have to be sifted and sorted in the early months of marriage. That is why marriage has been described as love with your eyes open. That is why marriage moves love along a notch, from the intoxication of the heightened emotional euphoria of engagement at its best, to the more mundane, realistic, rich and deeper experience of love-in-action, giving love at cost to yourself, giving love when it hurts, sacrificing number one's desires for the well-being of the loved one.

Disenchantment

This, of course, is where we feel the pinch of love. One reason why friction fractures many marriages as soon as the first-blush euphoria of the honeymoon is over is that disenchantment settles in, like an uninvited parasite. It saps the relationship of hope and quickly turns to disillusionment. The chief cause of this disenchantment is self-centredness. We want our marriage to become an 'us' relationship, that 'we' where two 'I's' meet, fuse and blend. But putting that romantic theory into practice is anything but bliss. It requires a degree of self-renunciation for which few of us are prepared in the early stages of marriage.

The problem is intensified because marriage is not a relationship where one self-centred partner marries a partner who is totally selfless. No. Even in Christian marriage, one self-centred person marries another self-centred person. The result is an inevitable existential clash of wills that can be both frightening and painful. The worst that can happen is that the conflict is not resolved, and that the marriage disintegrates. The best that can happen, as we shall go on to observe, is that conflict becomes the anti-toxin that will eliminate self-centredness; the friend who will encourage *both partners* to be transformed into the image of Christ.

Imperfections

Everyone knows the theory that the person they plan to marry is imperfect. Few of us come to terms with the reality until half way through the honeymoon, or perhaps even as late as the fourth month of marriage. Then the realization comes not with the silent splendour and majesty of sunrise, but with the sky-rending terror of a thunderstorm. The terrifying shock is two-fold: there is the shock of absorbing the grim fact that your partner has preferences that are not only different from yours, but actively oppose yours. And there is the deeper shock: that you, yourself, have not been perfected by love. This comes as a rude awakening because when you fall in love, you become completely other-oriented rather than self-oriented. This beguiles you into believing that you are capable of giving yourself totally to another, capable of renouncing self. For a while, you are. After marriage, you discover that this self-renouncing image was nothing more than a mirage. Now reality stares you in the face: you and your partner are as sinful and selfish as the couple who sit next to you in the pew on Sunday. You face the choice that confronts all couples: to choose whether to insist on rights and privileges or to meet the challenge of marriage, to place the needs of the partner and the needs of the marriage higher on the list than one's own needs. Friction is the crisis point where you examine your relationship and decide either to allow it to lie in ruins, or to make the necessary running repairs.

Two more pressure points in the early days of marriage trigger off friction. The first is the togetherness-with-space syndrome; the second, the thorny question of role responsibility. We shall look at the each in turn.

Problems of space and togetherness

Before you are married, you long to be together. Even when you are apart, you think of one another, dream of one another, store aways snippets of news to share with the other when you meet. This mental togetherness is one of the delights of love. But it is misleading. It can lull you into a false concept of married love, the belief that happily married couples always do everything together: pray together, wash up together, relax together. Of course, the togetherness of marriage is vital. It fuses two people so that they become one. But few of us can maintain constant togetherness. Almost all of us need privacy as well as companionship. One of the challenges of the first phase of marriage is to experiment with togetherness and space and to learn to strike a balance that will meet the needs of both partners. The experimentation is vital: it is also one of the chief causes of conflict.

Alan and Jenny found this. After five weeks of marriage, Alan longed for space from Jenny. 'I want to pray on my own as well as with her. I want sometimes simply "to be" in a room on my own without her. I want to think my own thoughts sometimes without the inevitable question, "What are you thinking about?"' Jenny, on the other hand, wanted only one thing, to be with Alan all day and every day. The result, for them, was tragic. To his horror, Alan became violent and started beating his wife. His violence was an expression of the depth of his frustration.

Frustration need not have erupted in this frightening way. We shall go on later in this chapter to discover how, for Alan and Jenny, friction became the friendly policeman who held up his hand, stopped the flow of friction, and persuaded them to try life another way.

Role-responsibility

The role-responsibility crisis, too, can be resolved even though for many couples marrying today, it is the most pressing challenge of the early years.

Kay put it well. 'I come in from school where I've been teaching all day. Often Brian is already at home. But instead of peeling the potatoes or putting the meat on, I find him curled up in a chair enjoying a good book. It makes my really annoyed. We've agreed to share the chores, but it still feels as if I've got two jobs: teaching and running the home, while he's only got one: his profession.'

Most women marrying today choose to continue to pursue their career. When two people work full time and try to assume responsibility in the life of the church and try to make a wholesome marriage, Bible-style, the pressure on their time and emotions can be overwhelming. Many find their spiritual awareness dwindles, others find that time for communication is crowded out, some find that it is their sex life that suffers, a subject that we shall examine in a later chapter. A large number of couples give up the effort and settle for a mediocre marriage, an impoverished sex life, a second-rate experience of Christ. This is unnecessary because each crisis can be converted into an occasion for growth, as we now go on to observe.

Friction is a friend in disguise

The clashes of wills and personalities I have described in this chapter need not result in the collapse of the marriage. On the contrary, they can make a significant contribution to the relationship if handled wisely. Such conflict is like a powerful electric cable. It can destroy or it can bring light, hope and comfort. Conflict confronted with Christ can transform marriages. The crucial question is 'how?'

A fire detector

Karen, whom I mentioned earlier, changed from a doting fiancée to a nagging wife. Whenever someone changes as dramatically as this, there is always a cause as well as an effect. The problem is that often we focus on the effect: the nagging, the blaming, the irritability, the personality change, and we fail to trace the behaviour change back to its cause—in this case, the heartbreak of loneliness. The fault here lies, not only with Brian, the injured partner, but also with Karen herself. She nagged instead of being open with her husband by admitting, 'I'm lonely.'

The first thing we must learn, then, is to allow friction to play the part of a fire detector. A domestic fire detector raises the alarm with an insistent bleep. When the alarm sounds you search for the source of the trouble.

Friction is like that. It pushes you into searching for the source. 'Why am I acting like this? Why am I bad-tempered, acting as though I were against my partner rather than on his side?' 'Why is my partner acting in this way? What is the need that underlies the negative behaviour?' Deal with the real need and you solve the real problem. React to the negative behaviour and you perpetuate the problem because nagging invites a negative response: more nagging, and so a vicious circle is drawn.

The friend that wounds

Friction is the friend, then, who invites us to recognize and express the real hurt gnawing away inside us: loneliness, displacement, unrealized expectations, unmet needs. Friction is the friend who whispers, 'Put yourself in your partner's shoes. Take a look at life through their perspective. Try to feel how they feel. Meet their hidden, unexpressed needs as a sign that you are committed to them in love.' Friction may wound. If often does. But as the writer of Proverbs says, 'Faithful are the wounds of a friend.'

The wounds inflicted by friction are an occasion for calmness and objectivity. They do not mean that your marriage is hurtling to a horrendous and inevitable end. Treated wisely, they could result in a deeper understanding of one another. Questions like these might hasten that growth in understanding:

What is causing the pain? How can we work together to seek to alleviate that pain? How must I change in order that the root of the problem is removed? Should I adjust my expectations of marriage or my partner? Are they too high? Am I overburdening my partner by demanding that all my needs should be met by him/her? Am I clamouring for all my needs to be met instantly? What changes can we make in our lifestyle to ensure that our marriage is mutually need-satisfying? Ask your partner, 'How would you like *me* to change to make our marriage more satisfying for you?'

If you are to respond to these questions openly and honestly, you have to oil the wheels of marital communication, a subject we examined in Chapter 5 and 6.

A trainer

I had to break off my work at this point to drive my husband to a meeting. When I came back, I paused to make myself a drink before taking up work again. When I walked into the kitchen I was horrified. I had left it neat, tidy and clean. My husband had since been there and left a bowl full of un-washed crockery in the basin. I was irritated. In my mind, I gave him a good telling off. Suddenly, a little voice inside me whispered, 'He's busy. You've got to forgive him.' I laughed. Friction is the friend that prompts us to forgive, the trainer who takes us through the elementary stages of this essential skill. Without forgiveness, love wilts, then dies. Without forgiveness we become embittered against our partner.

Friction also trains us to let go of our self-centredness. Friction in the first few years confronts us with our innate self-centredness, the absorption with self that creeps into marriage like woodworm creeping into furniture, causing it to rot and crumble.

Friction is the trainer who takes us through our paces even in the first phase of marriage. It shows us that although habits and preferences are well formed they are never so deeply ingrained that they cannot be changed. They can be changed and in certain circumstances they must be changed for the sake of the well-being of the marital relationship and of the partner. Friction shows where we must modify our behaviour, renounce self, and change certain habits and living patterns because our partner's wholeness and happiness matter to us more than our own. Friction under-lines the fact that the cost of love is extremely high.

The reformer

Friction is the friend who reforms us. Alan and Jenny, whom I have already introduced into this chapter, discovered this. As they each confessed their selfishness over the togetherness-with-space crisis and as they each responded to the other's question, 'How would you like *me* to change?' their love and understanding of each other deepened; a desire to change was born. As Alan expressed his need for space and solitude, not angrily or in a way that caused Jenny to feel rejected, but with gentleness and tenderness, Jenny recognized that he was not wanting to be apart from her because he had ceased to love her but because he wanted to deepen his prayer life. I heard them explore ways of ensuring that Alan's need for space was met. It was Jenny who suggested, 'Why don't we go home and clear out all the junk from the spare room? Then you could have a den all to yourself.'

The paradox was that when Alan recognized that Jenny was anxious to meet his need, at cost to herself, he needed less time on his own, not more. His love for Jenny had increased so that he was anxious that his need for solitude did not encroach on her need for closeness and companionship. It was Alan who thought aloud, 'How can we work it so that my times of solitude coincide with your activities: shopping, seeing friends?' The end result of the crisis was not the demise of love but a reformed lifesyle which cemented the affection that still binds them together.

And conflict (over role-responsibility) persuaded Brian and Kay to reform. When Kay poured out her resentment in front of Brian, at first he defended himself. 'I also have needs. I *need* to put my feet up when I come in from work.' Later, they both confessed their selfishness: Kay confessed her unrealistic expectations of Brian and he confessed the laziness that strapped him to the chair when he could have been helping with the chores. The asked themselves the vital question: 'How can we redefine our roles so that we each take responsibility for one-and-a-half jobs?' They adjusted their lifestyle accordingly. The reformation renewed their love.

That is not to say the problem is solved for ever. I have little doubt that Brian will drop back into his thoughtless, careless ways again, and it would not surprise me if Kay, martyr-like, assumes more responsibility for the home than this new agreement demands. Conflict will raise its head again. When it winks at them, they must take stock once more, laugh, and admit: 'Failed again. But we can do it. We will do it because we love each other; we are for each other, not against each other.'

Like road signs

When you are driving along a motorway at high speed and you see road signs, you slow down; you make a mental note that your concentration must increase. There may be men at work, an accident or roadworks. Friction in the first phase of marriage need be no more threatening than such road signs. It can keep you on the alert. It can persuade you to negotiate your marriage with concentration and care. It can work for you; it need not work against you. Viewed in this way, though friction will not be painless, it will be an adventure. As you work through it, stage by stage, you will adventure into the middle phase of marriage having learned some vital lessons; lessons that will stand you in good stead as you seek to be a master-driver not just of the marital relationship, but of the Christian family also.

9

Three Crises:
Pregnancy, Parenthood
and the Empty Nest

How a couple makes the transition from the euphoria of falling in love to the first phase of marriage, 'love with its eyes open', largely determines how that couple will cope with the second big crisis of marriage, the conception of a child. And how the couple adjusts to parenthood largely determines whether they will enjoy or endure the next major crisis of marriage: the departure of the grown-up children from the home, the phase of marriage when husband and wife are alone again.

In this chapter I propose to place the spotlight on these three pressure points: pregnancy, parenthood and the empty nest, to highlight some of the reasons why couples feel pressurized and to suggest how the head-on collisions can enrich the relationship, further the growth of love and deepen the couple's understanding of one another.

Pregnancy

The advent of the first child equals upheaval. Even if pregnancy is a much-longed-for event, the adjustments required of both partners can put a strain on each and on their relationship. This strain is superimposed on the stress we noted in the last chapter, the need newly-weds have of establishing a marital relationship that satisfies both partners spiritually, socially, sexually, emotionally and intellectually. Usually it is while the couple are still experimenting with degress of availability, still making the transition from the intoxicated, heightened emotions we sometimes call love to that deeper, richer, longer-lasting but more mundane manifestation of love, marriage, that pregnancy occurs. The consequence is chaos. As we shall go on to observe, this chaos, like an orchestra's tuning-up can resolve into harmony. But first we must ask what causes the cacophony of pregnancy.

Problems of pregnancy for the wife: hormonal, physical and psychological changes

One reason is that the hormonal changes that take place in the wife's body during pregnancy can cause considerable discomfort. She might become weepy or irritable, be plagued by morning sickness or feelings of nausea that spoil much of her day, be overcome by feelings of fatigue that leave her listless and lacking in vitality. These symptoms create anxiety and a loss of sense of well-being: they sometimes spill over as whining or petulance.

As the months wear on, the shape of the wife's body changes. The growing bump perturbs some women making them anxious and fearful. 'Am I still acceptable to my husband now that I'm a shapeless bundle?' She might look in the mirror and loathe the reflection. 'Will I ever again regain my figure? Are people laughing at this changing me?'

Self-doubt may increase for more subtle reasons. The mother-to-be often doubts her ability to cope with motherhood, worries because the maternal instinct is not as strong in her as it seems to be in some young wives, worries about the appropriateness of giving birth in a world as topsy-turvy as the one we live in. The pregnant woman also faces the challenge to resign her job for the sake of her husband and child. This renunciation equals a degree of loss that must not be minimized. It is costly. At the same time she might lose all interest in sex.

Pregnancy, for the wife, is a period of transition and stress as well as a period of mysterious joy. Her needs must be understood by her husband.

Problems of pregnancy for the husband: a series of changes

But pregnancy is not only a pressure point for women; it is bewildering for husbands too. The husband's needs must be met as faithfully as the wife's because the father-to-be faces a series of challenges: to understand this wife who is changing emotionally and physically, to come to terms with changing circumstances. One young husband explained how vulnerable he felt as he watched his wife change: 'My wife's not like herself at all. She snaps my head off if I can't read her mind. I'm finding it really hard to cope. I want to help her but I've never travelled this way before. I'm a novice. How do I read her needs and meet them? How do I show her that I want to understand her turmoil and alleviate it? How do I express love in a way she can understand? I don't want to retaliate when she's irritable but I find myself doing just that out of self-defence. I'm on unfamiliar ground, crossing an uncharted sea. I need help.'

The husband is not only confronted by a changing wife; there are other challenges like new expenses: a pram to be bought, nappies and miniature-sized clothes to accumulate, a nursery to be created or decorated. He may realize that the house is too small for an addition to the family, worry about the financial implications of the loss of his wife's salary, suffer sexually if his wife refuses to have intercourse or loses interest in physical intimacy.

Where one or both partner's needs remain unmet, conflict erupts in the form of bad temper, disagreement, blaming, accusing or in an emotional withdrawal from one another.

Parenthood

At the end of the prolonged waiting period another time of testing has to be faced: parenthood. Now the couple face the challenge of negotiating the many phases of their offspring's growth: babyhood and toddlerhood, childhood and the teenage stage. Parenthood is about challenge, change, growth in maturity. During these years the marriage either ripens, so that in the autumn of marriage, when the children have left to spread their own wings, the marriage bears all the glory of an Indian summer; or the marriage withers and decays, like a bad apple, from the inside out. Whether the marriage mellows or rots depends largely on how the couple copes with conflict during these critical years.

Conflict during the first phase of parenthood erupts for a variety of reasons. The chief one is the impact the arrival of the baby makes. Babies bring joys. Like the turmoil, they bear no resemblance to the size of the one round whom they resolve. But babies bring problems too. The biggest problem at first is the separation problem. For months, maybe years, the couple have been working at intimacy, experimenting with mutually need-satisfying degrees of togetherness. Suddenly this work is arrested by the inevitable separation that a baby brings: emotional separation, psychological separation, social separation.

Separation

The sheer helplessness of a tiny baby makes him a totally absorbing hobby. Life for a mother becomes a ceaseless round of breast-feeding or bottle-sterilizing, nappy-changing, nappy-washing, baby-bathing, baby-walking, baby-playing. Time for oneself and one's husband evaporates. As one young mother expressed it, 'I never sit down 'till 9 o'clock at night. Then I'm exhausted.'

This is not only frustrating for the wife, it is irksome for the husband too. During this phase of parenthood, it is not uncommon for a husband to feel neglected, to become resentful, even jealous of his clamouring child. He might compete with the infant for his wife's attention. He might hit out at his wife verbally, even with physical violence. Or he might withdraw from her, over-busy himself in his job or even reach out to another woman for the emotional support that his wife fails to give. 'If *she* won't satisfy my needs, I'll take them elsewhere.' 'If *they* don't want me, I'll jolly well show that I can cope without them.'

Loss

While the husband wrestles with powerful emotions like these, his wife may be smarting, suffering a series of losses that create a void in her life and that she feels increasing as the demands of parenthood mount up. Some 80% of women suffer from 'the blues' in the first ten days of parenthood, and 10% of these suffer prolonged periods of depression. This loss of energy and a clear perspective on life is matched later by the realization that parenthood also means a loss of financial independence for the wife that she might find humiliating. As one young mother put it, 'I find it really hard, having once earned a good income of my own, to ask my husband for money—even to buy him a birthday present.' There is also the loss of the companionship of colleagues, the healthy male-female interaction that most jobs afford, the loss of identity that is attached to the defined role of a job and a loss of status since there is a stigma attached to mothers who give up work for the sake of their children. Some wives feel the effect of this social stigma so keenly that they lose all sense of purpose in life.

Alongside all these losses comes a yearning on the part of the wife for adult conversation. When her husband arrives home from work, she demands his attention, clamours for news and forgets that he is weary from a day's work and needs solitude, space to unwind, the opportunity to put his feet up or to have forty winks in front of the television.

New needs

The challenge of the first phase of parenthood is the challenge to dovetail two sets of insecurities and fatigue into each other so that both partners nurture and heal each other's hurts rather than inflict each other with further wounds. This gargantuan task demands a high degree of maturity, sensitivity and unselfishness. Christlikeness at this stage of parenthood is not rushing off to prayer meetings, Bible studies and church services: it is recognizing the deep-seated needs of your partner and meeting them. Unless these needs are met, the husband will become over-whelmed by a wife who seems to him an ever-complaining, nagging woman. The wife will feel totally rejected by a husband who fails to recognize that gadgets, a luxury home and babies do not compensate for the lack of spouse-love, that rejection by the one you love is the most damaging wound you can inflict on another.

I am not advocating that parents of babies abstain from fellowship. They need the support of the body of Christ. I am saying that the arrival of babies presents a crisis in the life of the couple, a crisis that clamours for a change in the dynamics of the relationship. How the couple nudges its way through this crisis determines whether the inevitable conflict will become a servant or a master.

Parents of teenagers

At the toddler stage, constant demands siphon off energy: a barrage of questions all day, bedtime battlegrounds, broken nights. When toddlers become teens struggling to discover their own identity, the demands on the parents do not diminish. They simply change.

A relationship that fails to resolve the conflicts created by child-rearing at the early stage of parenthood crumbles as teenagers challenge, rebel, question and clamour for an ever-increasing degree of autonomy. The husband, reflec-ting on the battles he had with his mother when he was a teenager, sometimes sides with his teenage son and openly opposes his wife. The wedge driven between husband and wife widens the already-existing gap between them. Conflict then becomes, not a parent-teen crisis, but a clash of spouse personalities, wills and perception. At this stage of marriage, this is as potentially dangerous as dropping a match in a box of fireworks. If, at the same time, the spouses have learned to live parallel lives: the husband preoccupied with reaching the top rung of the professional ladder, the wife absorbing herself in the children's round of school and hobbies, in the church or neighbourhood or if she has returned to her own career, the situation is even more explosive. One or both parents may have taken the marriage for granted. Nagging and accusing may erupt because they are forced to come to some common conclusion about what limits to set of their offspring and how to enforce them. As the sparks fly over a reasonable curfew time or whether the wife should stay up until her daughter comes in after a party, neither partner realizes that something far more serious is happening here than quarrelling. Each partner is losing touch with the other's inner world: the world where the husband worries about the heavy responsibilities he shoulders at work, the world where the wife feels jaded alongside her attractive daughter, where she is full of anxiety about the future: life without her children and worse, old age. This loss of contact lies at the root of much conflict at this stage of marriage though it may be camouflaged by teenage traumas.

The empty nest

Despite all the pain of parenthood, by the time the offspring are ready to adventure into life independent of the parents, the empty nest presents just as many problems as the truculent toddler or the rebellious teenager. Emptiness equals loss. As one woman put it to me, 'I'm thrilled that my daughter has settled into university so happily but her

empty chair is awful. And so far, I daren't go near her
bedroom. It just reminds me that she's not here, not coming
in for supper tonight.' Or as one father expressed it when
his daughter left home to take up her first teaching post,
'When I saw her bedroom furniture being loaded into the
van, I felt tears well up in my eyes and a lump come to my
throat. "This is it, I thought to myself. Final. She's really
gone."'

Gone. Left. Final. These words describe the loss both
parents experience, albeit in different ways. Each needs
the other to come to terms with the loss of all that has been.
Each needs the other to come alongside them with understanding, compassionate love so that both can unclench
their fists from the past and hold out open palms to receive
whatever the future holds for them. Whether a couple ever
reaches this stage of acceptance depends on the maturity
with which they greet conflict, that 'friend' whose visits are
no less frequent now than they were twenty years earlier
before number one announced his arrival.

Enriched by conflict

Parenthood will never be conflict-free. As in marriage, in
general, so each period of parenthood is punctuated by an
inevitable intertwining of joy and pain. Many couples would
testify that the challenge presented by parental conflict can
be intimacy-enhancing not intimacy-destroying. How can
couples ensure that conflict in parenthood is constructive,
intimacy-enriching and not destructive? How can couples
ensure that when the children have flown from the nest,
and they are left alone perhaps for the first time for over
twenty years, their relationship is not as stale and musty as
summer clothes stored in a case all winter? How can head-
on collisions and submerged rumblings be used constructively?

Express the hurt not the anger

In the last chapter, we observed that anger is a reflex action that confronts us with a choice: to ventilate feelings inappropriately or to channel them so that they enrich our relationships. Most anger is born from hurt. But it is easier to express anger than pain. If I am angry with someone I love, my anger pushes them away and prevents them from hurting me more. If I express my hurt, they are capable of trampling on that pain and intensifying it. Even so, it is when we remove the masks and reveal the inner hurt that conflict enhances relationships.

Andy and Rachel found this as they worked through a backlog of pain. Andy's redundancy coincided with the birth of their first child leaving Andy resourceless and ill-equipped to cope with Rachel's maternal blues.

Before Rachel became pregnant, they used to enjoy working for God together, they enjoyed each other's company, they were gentle with each other. But pregnancy was not a pleasant experience for Rachel and she envied other young mums who seemed to blossom whenever they were pregnant. When she was overtired, which was most evenings, she would find fault with Andy and accuse him of not helping her in the home even though she knew he was under pressure at work.

When Andy was made redundant, she felt sorry for him, but she was angry too. He had made big mistakes and she would frequently remind him of these. On top of these accusations she would blame him: that he was no longer the spiritual giant he used to be, that the garden was neglected, that their home was not freshly decorated like the neighbours'. This angry blaming would pour out of her from time to time, like water from the spout of a kettle that has been left on the gas too long. And Andy would withdraw into his own world: tinker with the car in the garage, hide behind the crossword in the newspaper or sit glued to the television.

By the time their second child was on the way, both had

developed the habit of spitting out hatred rather than expressing love. They feared that their relationship was irreconcilable, so they sought help. When we examined the nature of the conflict, the friend who drove them to seek running repairs for their fast-rusting relationship, we focused, not so much on the anger, as on the underlying hurt.

When Rachel replaced accusatory phrases like, 'You never help me bath Jonathan', 'You never offer to look after him so that I can have a Quiet Time', with, 'I feel so frustrated because motherhood seems to be a seven to eleven job leaving me no personal space for prayer', 'I feel really frightened sometimes that I'm becoming a non-person, unable to make adult conversation, a domestic cabbage', the whole situation changed. Conflict put its finger on a vital lesson: what must be voiced is not anger, but hurt. Hurt can be healed. Expressed frustrations can be dealt with. But most people flee from the furnace of their partner's fury. Andy and Rachel learned through the hard school of conflict, to be real, to expose their pain to one another so that the other could understand, identify with the need and begin to meet it. Andy was able to tell Rachel that he needed her respect and trust. Rachel was able to voice her need for constant reassurance that she is loved for who she is, not for what she can do. The result was that their intimacy deepened.

Express real care

At first, Andy felt incompetent to handle the change in Rachel's approach. When she was angry, he knew he had either to fight for survival or flee for safety. When she reached out for his help he had to learn a new art: that of identifying with her pain and giving her solidarity in the pain. He had never come alongside anyone in need like this before. He had to improve his ability to listen to his wife; to hear, not just the words that left her lips, but the underlay of feelings beneath the words. He had to refuse himself permission to jump in with judgemental comments; 'You've got a lovely home. Fancy being resentful about being here all day bringing up our beautiful baby boy.' Andy gradually learned to put himself in Rachel's slippers, look at life from her perspective, emphasize, understand and act appropriately. As he offered her cherishing and unconditional love, Rachel's fears about her value were reduced. As he worked hard at remembering wedding anniversaries, birthdays, *un*-birthday presents, and taking her out for a meal from time to time, Rachel's complaining declined. She felt cherished.

Andy had to work at this time-consuming loving. It did not come naturally. Neither did it come easily to him to clarify rather than to assume that he had read the situation accurately. But out of his desire to express care for Rachel, gentleness was revived. He would try to remember to check whether he had understood correctly, 'Do you mean...?' 'Are you saying...?', 'If I were in your shoes I might feel..', 'I sense you're feeling...'

Pray

With the revival of gentleness and the determination to work at the love that ran like a hidden vein through their relationship came the renewed desire to pray: separately and together. Like many couples, Andy and Rachel admitted that they had neglected to claim the benefits promised to the twos and threes who pray together. Like many other couples before them, it was conflict that pushed them back into the prayer cycle which resulted in them drawing closer to one another as they reinstated Jesus as the focus of their relationship.

Examine priorities

And it was conflict that pushed two more friends of mine into the examination of their priorities which resulted in a marriage enriched. These friends, Phil and Christine, had two delightful children under four. When they met at university they had enjoyed attending church together and leading the youth group together. These Christ-centred activities continued in the early days of marriage. Then the first child arrived, clipping Christine's wings.

Phil, however, continued the ceaseless round of activities. He is a go-getter. He enjoys his responsible job. He has sufficient stamina to play squash regularly, attend two services on Sunday, lead the youth group and a mid-week Bible study group. But these activites take up four evenings every week. Christine goes out to Young Wives on one of the other evenings and often babysits for friends on another. On the remaining free evening, they try to entertain friends or relatives. Thus togetherness time is eroded.

When their marriage, like a ragged garment, began to fall apart at the seams, they stopped to make some essential stocktaking. Conflict forced Phil to examine his priorities. As he did so, he recognized that his weekly timetable was implying that work came first, church next, sport next and his wife and family last. Christine, too, scrutinized her priorities and was forced to acknowledge that her weekly routine was giving a similar message: children first, house-work next, Young Wives next, husband last. Conflict taught them two profound lessons: first, neglect of your partner and of the relationship is dishonouring to God; second, it takes time to make a marriage. When one or both partners becomes preoccupied with work, children, television, the church, sports, hobbies, friends or relatives, the marriage will suffer. Like Walt Disney's lovable character, Jiminy Cricket, conflict will fly into the situation to challenge, convict and confront.

The conflict that once threatened to divide Phil and Christine became the adhesive which bound them together when they learned to turn their list of priorities on its head. They both try now to put God first, the marriage (therefore one another's needs) next, children, third, and everything less finds its pecking order after that. This involved severe pruning of legitimate activities, the recognition that over-busyness prises partners apart. Overbusyness crowds out leisurely sex, denies couples time to communicate, creates short-fused tempers, banishes meaningful prayer. Conflict persuaded them to avoid this trap and instead to give one another qualitative time. When you give another your time you communicate an unspoken message, 'I care about you.'

Set clear goals

Andy and Rachel, Phil and Christine, like ourselves, are discovering the value of setting aside regular times to evaluate the relationship by asking questions that will result in clear goal-setting:

1. What are my current needs? How would I like my partner to meet them? Am I being reasonable?
2. What does my partner need from me? What can I realistically give?
3. Where must these needs be met through others?
4. If marriage is to become our high-priority commitment, what activities must be pruned back?
5. What steps can we take together to ensure that our intimacy is not blocked through pregnancy or parenthood, but enhanced?

Such questions facilitate short-term and long-term goal-setting and enable couples to search for ways to achieve these goals. The going is not always easy, but the resulting relationships grow as they are held together by the developing mutual understanding and care.

Acknowledge the changes in each other

I was once speaking to a woman about the tensions threatening the happiness of her marriage. She looked up at the window and groaned: 'There goes the source of all my problems.' Outside, her retired husband was pacing up and down the garden waiting to walk her home. 'He's like my shadow; never leaves my side. He thinks I'm still the naïve "little girl" I was when I married him. But I'm not. I've grown up. I don't need a father figure any longer.'

That woman put her finger on one of the crisis points of marriage in the later years: the failure of the spouse to recognize that the dynamics of the relationship have changed; the failure of both to do anything about this need for further adjustment.

The responsibilities thrust on us by God through parenthood hasten our personal maturity. We grow up. We have to. With increased maturity comes a shift in the nature of our need-love. The challenge of the later years of marriage, the empty nest, is not simply the challenge to come to terms with the departure of the offspring; the challenge of this stage of marriage is also to pinpoint where changes have taken place in each partner and to adjust the relationship accordingly so that both may continue to grow. The further challenge is to go on, in the light of this information, to fulfil our primary function in life: giving our partner in marriage a sense of security, providing for their physical welfare, placing them at the centre of our loving, drawing out their full potential so that these years are not wasted years but rather become the peak of personal and marital creativity.

It is our personal experience that conflict was the comforter who made us aware of such changes in our own lives: changes that had taken place within each of us and that needed to be reflected in our growing relationship. (I use the word comforter here in the biblical sense; like the Holy Spirit, one who not only consoles us in our sorrows but who also afflicts us in our complacency.)

It was the tyranny of pent-up frustration followed by prolonged depression in me that eventually highlighted the problem: that my needs had changed midstream and that neither David or I had been wise enough to recognize this nor to change our behaviour accordingly. I have described elsewhere (in *We Believe in Marriage,* Marshall, Morgan & Scott, 1982) how, for us, this conflict was a turning point; how it catapulted our marriage into growth, how it deepened our love and understanding of one another, how it over-hauled our entire relationship enabling us to emerge from the experience stronger and more resilient than before.

Our nest is now empty. We feel the loss of our adult children acutely. But our marriage is not dead; it is very much alive. We look back on our relationship and marvel that the conflict that once seemed to threaten the founda-tions of our lives served only to sharpen our perspective: our understanding of marriage, relationships, love and one another. Conflict has changed us. We are increasingly aware that, like the skilled sculptor we met in the summer, conflict is chipping away the inessentials so that, like pieces of a mosaic, we are more able to slot into one another's lives, more capable of slotting into the lives of others to take our place as parts of the body of Christ, better-shaped to settle into the cement of God's love. The faithful hand that did the reshaping was that uncomfortable companion: conflict.

10
Two More Clash Points:
In-laws and Money

It was the last week of term and I was looking forward to a long weekend at my fiancé's home before spending the Easter holiday with my parents. The phone rang. My father was distressed. 'It's your mother, Joycie [his pet name for me]. She's very poorly at the moment. I—I'm not coping very well on my own.'

'Don't worry, Dad. My lectures have finished. I'll get permission to leave early. I can be home tomorrow lunchtime.'

I went back to my room and started flinging clothes, books and files into a case. 'Better ring David. Tell him the weekend's off.'

David expressed his annoyance by giving me the cold, silent treatment. That hurt. 'He knows my mother's a semi-invalid. She needs me. This'll be my last holiday with them before we get married. Surely he won't grudge them that?' I felt trapped between two loyalties: fiancé who wanted me and ailing parents who needed me. Should I go home on the first possible train or go to David as planned?

Conflicting loyalties within marriage cause constant quarrels. Why do these problems arise? How can such conflict contribute to the upbuilding of marriage? These questions occupy the first part of this chapter.

The in-law problem: two women compete

In marriage, conflict usually erupts between the bride and her husband's mother. 'I find my mother-in-law really intimidating. She's a powerful woman. Quite often, she'll ring me up and as much as tell me what a terrible wife and mother I am. Nothing I do is right. The trouble is that when she's been accusing me down the phone for long enough, I begin to believe her. Then I get really upset. Maybe she's right? Maybe I should never have married her son? Maybe he and the children would be better off without me?'

'They call themselves Christians, those two—my daughter and her saintly husband. But do you know what they did last Christmas? They didn't even invite me to spend the day with my grandchildren. "We feel it's important to spend Christmas just as a family on our own", they said. So I was condemned to spend Christmas in my bungalow—alone. I know who's fault it is. Hers. I mean, my son would never shut the door on his poor old mother. He's always been such a good boy.'

Such problems between daughter-in-law and mother-in-law usually erupt because one feels threatened by the other and therefore each competes with the other. They may vie with one another for the same man's attention. Alternatively, they may recoil from one another to avoid disruptive relationships.

This in-law problem is accentuated whenever newly-weds are forced to set up home under the same roof as either set of parents. Newly-weds needs the freedom to experiment with a new marital lifestyle, to quarrel, to create a distinct, autonomous unit, to adjust to one another's foibles. When they set up home with either sets of parents, good all-round relationships cannot be established without a struggle. Moreover, the nesting instinct in women is so strong that you set the scene for trouble whenever you ask two women to share the same kitchen. It calls for more maturity and give-and-take than most of us possess.

Underlying pain: the cost of letting go

The tragedy about the in-law is that few parents set out to disrupt their children's marriages. Their inbuilt longing is to go on supporting their off-spring; to express love. Crises arise because the dividing line between support and intrusion is thumbnail thin. One can easily be interpreted for the other. Thus a well-meaning mother-in-law leaves a larder full of food for the newly returning honeymoon couple. The enraged bride reacts: 'This is *my* home, not hers. How dare she organize my kitchen before I've even got back from honeymoon.'

There is another reason why these relationships frequently rupture. At the stage of life when their children marry, parents, especially mothers, need their children far more than their children need their parents. The sense of loss is acute. Whenever I speak to groups of middle-aged to elderly couples about the need to let their children go, I read the same dismay and fear on their faces that I detect in my own heart. Perhaps to let your children go is *the* most costly challenge of parenthood; perhaps that is why pain as well as joy is evident at most weddings?

Some newly-weds sense these feelings of loss and try to compensate for them by allowing themselves to be over-attached to their parents even after they have married. Some are afraid of incurring their parents' wrath or displeasure, and therefore fail to make the transition from the dependency of childhood to the autonomy of marriage. Where one spouse remains in any such bondage to their parents or where partner-love fails to transcend love for parents, the marriage may be wrecked by the in-law problem.

The need: a complete break with the past

The need for married couples is space. This space should not be just a physical one, but a spiritual and psychological one also. This involves change, especially where parents have enjoyed being the central reference point, even the focus of their child's life. After marriage the partner must be given that focal place, not parents.

Where mother-in-law is a widow, or a divorcée, this detachment and displacement is extra hard. Nevertheless the second, invisible, umbilical cord by which mother and child are emotionally attached from babyhood, must be severed. Jesus calls this 'leaving' father and mother. Where there is no leaving there can be no proper 'cleaving': the deep, irrevocable, unbreakable union between man and wife cannot be forged.

Marriage needs a clean break with the past because marriage involves a change of ownership. (Thus, the bride's father *gives his daughter away*.) Marriage constitutes a change in authority structures, a change of commitment and a change of loyalties. After marriage, husband and wife must be free to venture into life together without being tied to parental apron strings.

The challenge: balance autonomy with care

That is not to say couples should neglect their parents. On the contrary, the challenge is to hold two principles in tension: to leave father and mother and to honour father and mother.

In other words, the challenge facing Christian couples today is to create a separate unit where they can set up a new nuclear family and at the same time to continue to express appreciation to both sets of parents by giving them tender loving care. 'To leave' does not mean 'to forsake', 'to break off the relationship', or 'to show no more interest' in parents. To leave means to create an entirely new unit where life may be tried your way, mistakes can be made and a unique pattern for marriage established. To leave also means to put one another first: before parents, job, friends, even before yourself. To leave means to cease to be dependent on your parents so that you and your partner can enjoy the free, mutual dependence that is one of the ingredients of marital love.

To leave means that from the security of this new love-nest, you shower love on your parents, not out of duty, but out of appreciative, unconditional love. You telephone them. You visit them. You invite them round. You remember birthdays and anniversaries. In short, you make it obvious that you care by meeting their needs without allowing them to invade your privacy. To keep this balance is very tricky. It is a challenge that exasperates many couples.

The model is Jesus. At the age of twelve (the Jewish equivalent of maturity), Jesus made it clear to his mother that it was no longer appropriate that he should be under her authority. 'Don't you know I must be about my Father's business?'

Here Jesus leaves his mother. But as he hangs on the cross, despite his own agony of spirit and body, he detects his mother's anguish, and meets her at the point of deepest need: 'Mother, behold your son.' Jesus cut himself free from his mother's apron strings but he never abdicated his filial responsibity to support, strengthen and love her.

This is the balance couples must seek to maintain: autonomy matched by care; independence laced with compassion; separation bridged by love-in-action.

Conflict: a means of grace

Conflict is the friend whose duty it is to bring marriages into alignment with this biblical pattern. But it is not always easy to recognize what is required of us as Val found.

Val's relationship with her mother-in-law is delicate at the best of times. When a letter arrived recently containing a five-pound note, 'For some vests for my wee grandson', Val became very angry. 'Fancy her sending money like that. She can't afford it on her pension. New vests indeed! I know why she's done it. She was grumbling the other day because I'm still dressing him in size 1 vests and she thinks he needs a bigger size. She's determined to get her own way like she always does.'

Val could have picked up the phone, given her mother-in-law a mouthful of her anger and their precarious relationship would have been gutted as by fire.

There is another way. Val will never change her mother-in-law but God can change Val if she will ask, 'What is it about me that can't cope?' Similarly, when we feel hurt or threatened, as determined to have our own way as our mother-in-law is to have hers, we must ask, 'Is this Christlike?' God often uses such potential conflict to place his finger on certain attitudes of ours that should find no place in citizens of the kingdom of God: pride, bitterness, resentment, lovelessness. (Love, according to Paul, is not rude, does not keep score of wrongs, always thinks the best of another.) When God turns our attitudes on their head so that we not only forgive our mother-in-law but try to understand and accept her also, conflict becomes a means of grace, refining us.

This work of refining, being changed into the likeness of Christ, is also promoted when we search for an answer to another question: How does my partner need to change?

At the beginning of this chapter, I used a personal illustration: the conflicting loyalties that tore me in two when I was engaged. The conflict that drove an ice-cold wedge between David and me that Easter convinced me of my need to sift priorities. What would happen after our marriage if my mother was taken ill? Would I always drop everything and go to her? Was I perhaps encouraging over-dependency on me, the only daughter, the one who had provided my mother with emotional support for many years?

When your partner is in turmoil, working through complex questions like these, they need understanding, prayer support and patience. It takes time to reach objective answers. Conflict becomes a means of grace when it draws these qualities out of you instead of the nagging, blaming and insecurity that rises to the surface in most of us at such times: the uncertainty that gives birth to this kind of comment: 'You're supposed to put me first, not her.'

A challenge to live objectively

Another question that begs to be answered at such times is this: What is this deadlock teaching us about our need to leave and to cleave? In what ways must we change to come more in line with the Bible's blueprint for marriage?

Conflict, confronted in this objective way, can highlight where specific changes in your timetable and attitude could benefit you, your partner and your marriage. Your parents' love and concern for you is ingrained. You might have to take the initiative in channelling this well-meaning love along avenues that are acceptable to you; to discover ways of freeing them to express their concern in practical, concrete ways without encroaching on your much-needed family time. This might involve confrontation. 'We really feel the need to have our holiday on our own this year.' Whenever there is a need for firmness, there is a parallel need to remember the Bible's exhortation: speak the truth *in love*. Whenever confrontation like this seems necessary for the preservation of your togetherness, make sure that your parents also understand another message: that you love them and want to work for their well-being also.

Barry and Sue found the challenge to live objectively a difficult one. They dreaded their first Christmas as a married couple. As Sue put it, 'I feel so resentful. Barry's parents are insisting that we spend Christmas Day at their place. But they're not Christians. Christmas, for them, means over-eating, over-drinking and piles of expensive presents. But if we were at my home we would all go to church together at midnight on Christmas Eve and Christmas Day would be a simple celebration of Christ's birthday. I'm really disappointed. I mean, my mum's the best friend I've got. I really miss her now that I'm married, and I desperately wanted to be with her on Christmas Day. Now I've got to wait till Boxing Day. It's awful. I don't get on with Barry's parents at all.'

'Barry's parents are insisting that we spend Christmas Day at their place.' That is a subjective reaction; the way it felt. The fact of the matter is that Barry's parents no longer have a right to insist. Barry and Sue must listen to the request, weigh it and decide together, before God, how they will spend Christmas. God, of course, expects us to refer to his word about such decisions and, as we have already seen, his clear instruction is: honour your father and mother. If this means anything, it means respect them, bring them joy, do all you can to express love through actions, hold them in high esteem because they, too, are persons loved by God. It does not mean, give in to every demand of theirs. Neither does it permit us to live selfishly, to let personal preferences rule our lives. When we learn to live objectively and to act lovingly towards someone, acting as if we loved them even in the absence of warm feelings, over a period of time a miracle happens. We find ourselves *feeling* kind, warm, loving.

A red light signifying 'change gear'

That is not to say the in-law problem suddenly disappears. It sometimes gets worse as the parents grow older and become more frail. After they have died, any neglect of them leaves a guilt-stain on your conscience. Conflict can be the red light that brings your relationship to a halt and challenges you to change gear; to try life another way. One 'new way' is to refocus, away from their bad points and on to their good points. 'What I like about your mother is...' 'What I like about your father is...' This positive approach, accompanied by a readiness to forgive your in-laws their faults and foibles in the same way as God forgives you, is healing. It could even create a Ruth-and-Naomi closeness. As one woman put it to me recently, 'I value my mother-in-law—really appreciate her. She has shown me how to grow old graciously. Despite all her trials she has not become embittered. Her dependence on God through thick and thin has deepened my faith.'

This relationship had not always been sweet but conflict persuaded this woman to put off the bitterness and put on an accepting attitude. It worked.

Money matters

Arguments over money frequently flare up between married people creating ripples of negative feelings, sometimes leaving deep scars. Why? How can these snarl-ups work for the relationship rather than against it? These questions will occupy the second half of this chapter.

Money and self-esteem

One reason why money causes conflict is that money is not simply a series of coins and pieces of paper that carry economic value. It is also one of the most sensitive areas of married life, a powerful symbol for care and an equally powerful symbol for contempt. If a husband is mean or irresponsible with money, his wife will feel personally affronted. If the wife is careless with the housekeeping, the husband will feel insulted. The psychological undercurrents accompanying most money matters can diminish our partner's sense of value and worth or it can strengthen it.

The truth of this was imprinted on my mind as I began to write this chapter. My husband, who knew I hoped to do some shopping in the market the next day, wandered into my study, having just been to the bank. 'Here's five pounds.' David held out a crumpled five-pound note. 'Five pounds? But that doesn't go anywhere these days and you know I'm going to Ripley market tomorrow.' 'Oh well! Have another.' He held out a second, crisp, new note. 'Will that be enough? You don't look very pleased. Well, how much *do* you want?'

By the time we agreed on a sum of money, I was feeling hurt because I sensed David had failed to understand me. It seemed as though he was being stingy. I felt demeaned, unappreciated, put down as a wife and housekeeper. The fact of the matter was that he had forgotten that one reason why I was going to the market was to stock up the freezer with meat and pies.

The treasurer

Some couples quarrel over money because they cannot agree over the fundamental question of who should manage the money. This happened to Nick and Gwen. Gwen's father always kept his finger on the financial pulse of their family affairs. When she married Nick she assumed that he would do the same. But Nick was useless with money and as disorganized as Gwen was. So bills dropped through the letter box and remained unpaid until reminder after reminder came. Gwen would grow anxious and worry at night. Bitter rows spoiled their relationship until she threatened Nick with divorce.

Mismanagement

Because both Nick and Gwen were totally disorganized about money matters, the little money they did have (they were living on a student grant) as badly mismanaged. It failed to work for them. From month to month they never knew whether they would have enough to feed themselves and their two children, let alone buy clothes for the two little girls.

Other couples mismanage money for other reasons. Advertisements on television encourage covetousness. They persuade us that we *must have* the latest gadgets and have them now. They persaude us that we will not be happily married without such seeming necessities. They push us into the belief that every married couple *needs* at least one sun-soaked holiday a year. That little fiend, the Access card, not only takes the waiting out of our wanting, it encourages us to overspend. It makes the impulsive buying that has been the downfall of many married couples an easy option.

The materialism most of us in the West are caught up in is frightening. Materialism has become our way of life, the cultural norm. We call 'wants' and 'keeping up with the Jones's' 'needs'. Instead of ignoring the sales 'bargains', we are drawn to them. Instead of turning our back on special offers, we fall for them and fill our cupboards with unwanted items that clutter our homes and cause more quarrels.

Personality clash

When a money-squandering partner marries a miser, the problems are not purely financial but emotional. Ted, the spendthrift, comes in proudly wearing his new coat that he bought for £10 in the sales. Joy, his thrifty wife, expresses her horror. 'But we haven't got £10 to spare. And anyway, it's a terrible colour. It doesn't even suit you.' The lasting hurt here will not be the £10 unwisely spent but Joy's hurt that her husband has wasted *their* hard-earned cash and not taken her needs into consideration. Ted, on the other hand, will feel humiliated by Joy's ticking off.

Self-centredness

Self-centredness is as much a killer disease as the plague used to be. The way we manage our money so often reflects the fact that self not God sits on the throne; that self is of greater importance than our partner's needs. So a husband buys an expensive boat, pursues a pricey hobby, or spends an inordinate amount at the sports centre each week. 'It's my right—I need it to unwind.' Or a wife will insist on costly weekly visits to the hairdresser without making reference to the family budget. 'I have to spoil myself sometimes.'

This self-centredness is worldliness. In the West today, money and possessions are status symbols. As someone living in a certain suburb put it to me recently, 'If you live in this road it means you've arrived.' But those who have arrived are prone to just as much conflict as the have-nots. A quarrel erupted between the man I've just mentioned and his wife: 'You've forgotten to switch on the burglar alarm again.' 'Oh, it doesn't matter at this time of day.' 'But what if someone breaks in—what about that antique table we bought last week?'

The have-nots face other pressures, like a certain friend of mine, the mother of three children. Her husband used to insist on moonlighting 'to buy a better house and new clothes for the children'. His wife used to complain to me, 'We hardly ever see him. When we do there are constant rows because he's always tired. I'd rather have a little house and just one set of clothes for the children and a husband who's a companion than all this extra cash.'

The use of money puts the co-partnership of marriage under a severe strain. It tests the couple's togetherness-capacity and poses a problem. Can you organize your life together in an orderly and efficient manner? Many couples are caught out by this. Though they were head-over-heels in love when they married, this intoxicating feeling makes no contribution to wise money management. It gives no clue about essential matters like how money should be spent and how much should be saved.

Conflict: the finger which points to the biblical norm

How can such conflict work for a couple, strengthening their love, not reducing it? Before we look for answers to this question, we examine a biblical perspective on money.

The Bible makes it clear that all our possessions are a trust from God (1 Chron 29:14).

Married couples therefore have a responsibility to manage God's money wisely, to be good stewards of the possessions with which he entrusts us. Jesus implied that good stewardship is something that is applauded by God whereas the mismanagement of money provokes his displeasure (Lk 19:11–26).

The New Testament makes it clear that taxes are to be paid and not avoided (Rom 13:6–8; Mt 22:15–22), that the accumulation of loans, being steeped in debt, is forbidden to the Christian and it exhorts us to be content with whatever the Lord chooses to give (Heb 13:5). Moreover, as Christians we are encouraged to explore the joys of generous giving (2 Cor 9:6–8). We are commanded not to rob God (Mal 3:8ff.).

Many of the quarrels that create conflict between Christians erupt because they have departed from this biblical norm. Conflict is the finger that pinpoints the discrepancy between the topsy-turvy standards of the kingdom of God and the worldly patterns of behaviour we married people slip into so easily.

I think of Tony and Pauline, for example. Tony had accumulated a series of serious crippling debts in his early twenties. Pauline resented the huge hole this made in his monthly pay cheque. She became bitter and sarcastic, accusing and condemning her husband. This conflict caused them to seek some counselling. Tony saw that, by changing his job, the debt could be paid off immediately, bringing the twin benefits of a sweeter relationship with Pauline and a more biblical lifestyle. Within months a new job prospect opened up that Tony took. I am not excusing Pauline's unsupportive behaviour. I am underlining the fact that conflict, if we listen to the underlying message it is trying to convey, can bring us into line with God's plan for our lives.

Shared responsibility

Or think back to Nick and Gwen whom I mentioned earlier in this chapter. Gwen was angry at Nick's incompetence. She laughed when I asked, 'Are you expecting him to be just like your father, only better?' By admitting that the demands she was making on her husband were unreasonable, conflict became the faithful friend who reminded her that if you put your partner on a pedestal or cherish unrealistic expectations of their role in the relationship, they can do only one thing: Fail.

Conflict over money brought Nick and Gwen to the solemn realization that something had to be done about this strand of their marriage; that Nick could not be expected to carry the money-management load alone, that they must share the responsibility. We therefore worked together on some basic ways forward:

1. Decide who will be the treasurer by asking, 'Which has a flair for finance?'
2. If neither are gifted in this way, agree to learn. Agree to learn together.
3. Agree on a policy.

An agreed policy

In order to agree on a policy, couples must work out a hypothetical budget. Pool your income. Make a note of your total earnings. Divide your expenditure into sections, under headings like these:

1. *Tithe*	Since the Bible makes it clear that we are not to rob God but to tithe our income, earmark God's slice first. Agree on a certain sum. Decide whether you will give one tenth of your total income, or one tenth after tax deductions. Discuss this with your partner.
2. *Taxes*	Since the Bible also commands us to return to the government their due, estimate your tax payment as accurately as possible.
3. *Everyday expenses*	It may not be easy to estimate running expenses at first, but over the months this will become clear. Under this heading include food, drink, heating, lighting, water, household goods, gifts, postage, telephone, clothes for the children. Everyday running expenses.
4. *Extraordinary expenses*	Car tax, car insurance, petrol, TV licence, holidays, leisure, entertainment, meals out. Leisure expenses.
5. *Home expenses*	Insurance, mortgage or rent. Rates. Furnishings. Decorating. Garden equipment. House repairs. Everything for the home.
6. *Saving*	Ask yourselves, 'What proportion of our income can we save/invest?' If you are living on a student grant or the dole that question

may seem laughable. But take it seriously. The day will come when saving should find a niche in your budget.

7. *Outstanding debts* If you *have* bought items on hire purchase pay these off systematically and regularly.

8. *Giving* Your tithe is your duty. Earmark some of your income for extra giving and experience the joy God pours in to generous givers.

There are three golden rules to remember. Ensure that your earnings exceed your expenditure. Let your spending be controlled, not impulsive, based on needs and not wants. Remember that God is not simply interested in the tithe, the 10%, but also what we do with the rest, the 90%.

A personal allowance: 'mine'

One of the reasons why couples come to verbal blows, if not physical violence, over money is that one partner, usually the wife, feels deprived, cheated. It is demeaning to have to ask your partner for every single coin, even to go to the Ladies. The eruption of this sort of conflict helps many to discover a workable plan that eliminates this problem. First, they estimate their budget. Each then works out what they think they need for the etceteras of life: hair-cuts, talcum powder, bus fares, clothes. They go on to agree on a personal allowance for both, a slice of income that each can call 'mine'. This can be given away, frittered away, or saved or spent without reference to anyone but God. This method has removed the steam from many a marital financial crisis. It makes the joint-account approach not only workable but fun.

11
Sex: A Subtle Weapon

A brave husband once wrote the following letter to his wife:

To my ever-loving wife,

During the past year, I have attempted to seduce you 365 times. I succeeded 36 times. This averages once every ten days. The following is a list of excuses made on the unsuccessful occasions:

We will wake the children	7	The baby is crying	18
It's too hot	15	Watched late night show	7
It's too cold	3	Watched early show	15
Too tired	19	Mudpack on	12
It's too early	9	Grease on face	6
It's too late	16	Reading Sunday paper	10
Pretending to sleep	33	We have company in the next room	7
Windows open—neighbours will hear	3	Your parents were staying with us	5
Your back ached	16		
Toothache	2	My parents were staying with us	5
Headache	26	Is that all you ever think about?	105
Giggling fit	2		
I've had too much	4		
Not in the mood	21		

Do you think you could improve our record this coming year?

Your ever-loving husband*

* Quoted by Jack Dominian, *Marital Breakdown,* Pelican, 1968, p.79–80.

That letter reminds me of another young married couple. 'What are the main pressure points in *your* marriage?' I asked them. They laughed. The wife summed it up in one word: 'sex'.

Or I recall the anguish of a couple who told me the story of their five-year-old marriage. 'Right from the start, even on our honeymoon, our sex life's been a complete shambles. My wife's never enjoyed an orgasm. If I stop to think about it all, it worries me silly. Bed is sheer relief, not for sex, but for the deep sleep which blocks out the nightmare of no sex.'

Stories of sex indifference in marriage, of monotonous sex, mediocre sex, or sex-withholding could fill several pages. They are a common phenomena in marriage. This is serious because the difference between a marriage where sex is mutually satisfying and marriage where one or both partners fail to find sexual fulfilment is the difference between a sun-splashed day in spring and a drab, grey-wet November day. Whether we like to admit it or not, sex in marriage colours everything. Sex even becomes a subtle, strategic weapon in the warfare conflict introduces into marriage.

In this chapter, therefore, it is my plan to focus on two questions that require an urgent answer. Why do couples quarrel over sex? How can such conflict be used creatively to turn sexual disharmony into sexual fulfilment?

Doing what comes naturally

The way marital quarrels sometimes cluster round sexual problems reminds me of the way maggots crawl over a chicken carcase. One reason for the problem is that couples marrying today are not only steeped in the media's box-office-appeal approach to sex but they have swallowed, unquestioningly, the big lie about sex that they hear there. One of these lies is the myth that sex is doing what comes naturally. Some couples who have swallowed this sliver of the truth depart for their honeymoon cherishing high hopes and expectations of the romantic first night, only to discover that mutually satisfying sex is an art form to be learned, not something that necessarily comes naturally or easily. A few couples are honest enough to admit this: 'The first night was a complete disaster. The other nights of the honeymoon weren't much better. In fact, we went straight round to our doctor when we got back. It's OK now but why didn't someone warn us that sex might be fraught with problems at the beginning?'

Satisfying sexual intercourse is an art form that, like any other art form, demands learning time. (It often takes a couple a whole year, sometimes much more, to establish good sexual rapport with one another.) This art form also requires patience, sensitivity and tenderness within an on-going, secure relationship.

Couples who remain ignorant of the fact that sexual adjustment in the early months of marriage is more the rule than the exception, who believe that a frustrating start to their marriage dooms them to a lifetime of sexual incompatibility, who feel cheated by initial sexual incompetence, frequently fall to quarrelling and even to physical violence. The underlying reason for these quarrels, as we shall observe later, is disillusionment.

Ignorance is bliss

Another reason why some couples encounter sexual problems at the beginning of their marriage is that they do not take the trouble beforehand to acquaint themselves with the anatomy of the male and female body, or to investigate the do's and don't's of sexual intercourse. Often, this educative lack stems from the firm belief that ignorance is bliss. It is not. This myth gives rise to untold psychological, emotional and even physical pain. It also results in bewilderment and strife.

Couples intending to marry owe it to one another to be reliably informed about conjugal sex. This does not mean they should imbibe the media's attitudes. It does mean they will absorb what the Bible says about sex, learn from its frankness that God does not want us to be embarrassed when we discuss intimacy, and bring their attitudes into line with his. They will also buy a good sex manual,* read it together, discuss it and, if possible, attend a course for engaged couples where sex is discussed in realistic and honest terms. They will acquaint themselves with certain facts: the positions most couples use to enjoy intercourse: the importance of foreplay, that mutually delightful activity that is a part of the ecstasy, not simply a warm-up before the game begins; the importance of the clitoris to the wife's enjoyment; the difference to be expected between the male and female approach.

The tyranny of statistics

Couples who base their understanding of sex in marriage on the media's sex propaganda fall prey to the tyranny of statistics: the false claim that 'successful sexual partners' enjoy a series of saucy sex jaunts every night.

The bride's mother reinforced this claim for one couple I know. She insisted on underlining that *well-adjusted* couples enjoy sexual intercourse every night. This is nonsense. A minority of couples do attempt to have intercourse most nights. The average couple, if statistics are to be believed, enjoy intercourse two or three times each week. And many couples, seeing sex as a vital strand of their marriage but only one strand, are completely satisifed with sex as an occasional treat, enjoying love-making only once or twice each month.

* A sex manual written by Christians that I recommend is *Intended for Pleasure* by Ed Wheat and Gaye Wheat (Scripture Union, 1977): Maxine David's *Sexual Responsibility in Marriage* (Fontana, 1969) is also excellent, though not written from a Christian perspective; my own books, *Two into One?* (IVP, 1981) and *Growing into Love* (IVP, 1982) discuss sexual matters frankly from a biblical perspective.

No one must dictate another's frequency pattern. No one else need know. The criteria for frequency should be established by the couple themselves in response to certain questions: How often does my partner want sex? How often do I need it? How can we put these two sets of needs and wants together to ensure that both are fulfilled? When couples fail to assess the situation in this way, sexual wrangles become an increasing problem resulting in the destructive score-keeping which led one embittered young husband to comment, 'We haven't had intercourse now for nine months and three days.'

The multi-orgasm myth

Articles frequently appear in glossy magazines extolling the virtues of sexual enjoyment for women. They go into great detail, instructing women in the art of achieving not one orgasm, but many orgasms during one sexual encounter. The implication is, to be successful and sexy, a multi-orgasmic experience is a must.

The consequence of such articles for many women who believe them and whose sexual experience does not match all they read is devastating. 'I don't know if you can understand how it feels when you read something like that, when for years you've been struggling to come to a climax and nothing happens. I ask myself the same question over and over again, "What's wrong with me? Why aren't I normal?" To feel sexless in a sex-saturated society is terrifying.'

Some of the conflict that arises over sex, then, is born of insecurity and deep hurt. The problem is that most of us prefer to protect that soft inner centre where life hurts. We keep even our loved ones out with a protective layer of anger or quarrelling, which, of course, aggravates the problem.

Simultaneous orgasm

It cannot be denied that simultaneous orgasm provides each partner, not only with simultaneous pleasure, but with a great sense of achievement. But to claim, as some do, that unless this split-second orgasmic experience is reached every time the couple are sexual failures, is nonsense. Such thinking is a pressure: a pressure to conform and a pressure to perform. But sexual intercourse was never intended to become a performance in which couples either succeed or fail. Sexual intercourse is God's wedding present to couples: a love language providing married couples with a method of communicating, albeit non-verbally, that most healing of messages: 'I love you. I care about you. I appreciate you.' This message can be communicated through the language of touch even though neither partner achieves an orgasm. In the absence of an orgasmic experience, who is to say that the couple have *failed* if each has communicated tenderness and love to the other?

Unrealistic expectations

Quarrels frequently arise between couples because their expectations are not met. The consequent so-called 'failure' threatens their self-esteem, and this sets in motion a partner-blaming cycle where sex becomes a tool to fight non-sexual battles.

This happened to Ron and Cynthia. They had been married for ten years when they decided to seek help for their fast-disintegrating marriage. They had slept together before they were married and looked forward to zestful sex after their wedding day.

During their honeymoon, Cynthia made it clear that she found sex nauseating. Ron was appalled. Why hadn't she told him before?

Over the years he tried to help her to enjoy sexual intimacy, a dimension of loving that was vital to him, but

Cynthia still insisted that, for her, sex was repugnant. Ron retaliated by criticizing his wife for almost everything: her lack of domesticity, her lack of interest in cooking, her failure to iron his clothes. 'I even have to cook my own breakfast,' he complained.

Cynthia's response to this was to belittle her husband so that he lost confidence, not only in his ability to be a successful sex partner, but in his ability to be the head of the home as well. Unknown to Ron, Cynthia read every glossy magazine she could lay hands on in an attempt to discover how to please her husband sexually. The more she 'failed', the more irritable she became. Unfortunately her irritability was expressed not as hurt, 'I wish I could get it right for your sake', but as anger. 'It's all your fault. You're too quick for me. You don't listen when I tell you what I like.'

The vicious circle that trapped Ron and Cynthia from the early days of their marriage onwards is all too familiar in many marriages. Sometimes it occurs because early sexual difficulties remain unresolved and these become the peg on which the couple hang all the other ambivalences about the marriage. At other times unresolved personality clashes are brought into the sensitive area of sexual relating and disrupt it. Either way, from this vicious circle radiates a great deal of marital contention.

An over-glamourized view of sex

It was as though Ron and Cynthia had been brainwashed. Both of them expected intercourse to be passionate· Hollywood-style romanticism. It had not occurred to them that sometimes sex is cosy, comfortable or lazy, at other times fun, while on occasions it is other-worldly, transporting both partners into ecstasies of delight. Ron and Cynthia had to learn to appreciate love-making in all its different expressions, not to devalue some forms of love-making.

Sex wrangles: an innocent sport

Ron and Cynthia also had to learn that their habitual bitter
verbal fighting over sex was destructive of each of them as
people as well as of their marriage. This came as a surprise
to them. Like many couples, they spent three hours or so
each night in front of the television. There they heard
couples quarrel over sex and took this to be the norm. It
probably is. That does not make it acceptable, nor does it
mean that sexual wrangles are an innocent sport.

On the contrary, Cynthia discovered that her criticisms
of Ron's love-making technique were wounding her husband, causing him to doubt his self-worth and his mascu-
linity; that her deliberate withholding of sexual intimacy
was causing him emotional and physical pain.

Ron, meanwhile, began to discover the effect his attitude
was having on Cynthia; that to call her 'cold' and 'frigid'
injured her; that she even believed his cruel jibes.

They discovered that such sex squabbles, far from being
the innocent sport all couples take part in, are a deadly
weapon which, when wielded, kills. They learned that
bickering over sex is a cruel, not an innocent, sport.

Standing on our rights

Cynthia seemed to believe that since sex for her was a
non-event, she had every right to make it difficult for Ron
to make love to her. This is not correct. When we marry, we
forfeit our rights, even to our own body. The Bible emphasizes that married couples should not defraud one another
sexually unless they do so for an agreed, limited period,
and for the sake of prayer. Failure to obey this biblical
injunction results in intolerable pain for at least one partner:
the pain of rejection. This pain gives birth to a disharmony
that percolates through to the entire relationship.

Both partners should always be in the mood

Another myth that worms its way into couples' minds is that unless both partners are 'in the mood', they should not attempt to have sexual intercourse. This attitude causes countless quarrels because one or other of the partners feels deprived or cheated.

But sexual intimacy is not just about responding to a fluctuating mood. Sex is an unselfish giving of oneself to one's partner. Both partners respond, not to personal needs dictated by mood, but to the unselfish desire that the loved one will be satisfied. '*She* will enjoy a climax tonight.' '*He* will be fulfilled whenever we make love even if I don't feel in the mood.' Couples who act as if they were in the mood often discover that their feelings catch up with their actions. It is one of the mysteries of life that in dedicating your will and your body to bring joy to your spouse, you receive pleasure for yourself also.

Sex roles

Yet another myth that needs exploding is that the husband should always take the initative in sexual activity. Some wives suffer unnecessary anguish because they are afraid to make the first move in love-making. If both partners agree that the role of intimacy-initiator may fall to either the husband or the wife, an aspect of relating sexually that needs to be discussed, then there is no reason why the wife should not make the first move. Couples need to find a time and a position and a technique that is comfortable, relaxing or exciting for them. Whether it bears any correlation to anyone else's sexual lifestyle really does not matter. God gave the gift of sex for couples to bring joy to one another in a way that bypasses words; in a way that is unique to each couple.

Sex can be compartmentalized

We have seen already in this chapter that sex cannot be compartmentalized. Sex colours everything. The reverse is also true. Everything else colours sex. Thus a couple who have been working too hard, depriving one another of companionship, communication, tenderness or sensitivity are unlikely to enjoy mutually satisfying sex. Similarly, a couple who have become neglectful of personal hygiene, the husband who fails to wash his feet at night, the wife who insists on sleeping in hair-curlers, the couple whose night attire has become shabby, might find this drabness and self-neglect reflected in their love-making. These factors may not give rise to brawls or open conflict. They may accumulate and contribute to the conglomeration of marital disharmony of which sexual non-relating is one part.

Biblical attitudes towards sex

Christian couples, I find, are often reluctant to discuss sexual conflict. One of the reasons for this is that many harbour unbiblical attitudes towards sex. Some think that sex is dirty, sordid or polluted. Others believe that sex is animalistic. Some feel Christians should only have sex if they intend to conceive a child. Others think sex is embarrassing, private, not something 'nice' couples talk about. Some still feel sex is a necessary evil, a part of the curse. These unbiblical attitudes spawn unspoken hostilities. These hostilities, in turn, produce severe sexual problems: frigidity, impotence, guilt; the sexual dysfunction that cripples couples' lives.

In my two books, *Two into One* and *Growing into Love,* I have tried to spell out the good news that sex is not dirty, nor is it a guilty secret. On the contrary, sexual intimacy was designed and created by the architect of the male and female body, God. He gave sex to married couples for their enjoyment, for their healing, for their completion. Man without woman is incomplete. Woman without man is incomplete. In the act of intercourse, they reunite. And God looks on, smiles and reflects, 'This is very good.'

Disillusionment

Disillusionment is a killer. As we have seen, one of the reasons why the incidence of marital breakdown in the West is so high today is because couples go into marriage with idealistic and unrealistic expectations of a relationship that two imperfect people cannot hope to match. This includes expectations about the sexual relationship.

Even in the most well-adjusted marriages, there are sticky patches that have to be worked at. 'I'm dreading my wife's second pregnancy. All those weeks of endless abstinence.' Even in the good patches, most couples achieve something short of heavenly harmony. Unless couples come to terms with these sober, light-of-day facts, they are doomed to despair. They will collide over sex because after a few years of incompatibility or so-called 'failure', the fear that their sexual technique is never going to improve will hold them in a firm grip. Such frustration and disappointment is to marriage what water is to stone; even if it falls only slowly, drop by drop, it succeeds eventually in wearing away the surface. Similarly, the stark realization that sexual dysfunction may not be an early-adjustment, transient problem, but a part of life, wears down good will and is another source of irritability and conflict.

Specific problems

Sexual problems in women

Certain sexual problems crop up frequently. They cause considerable distress and often give rise to sulks and strife. The first to be encountered by some is the pain some wives experience early on in marriage at the moment when their husband's penis penetrates the vagina. There are several possible reasons for this upsetting problem: the wife's hymen might be thick or unbroken (this can be stretched almost painlessly by a doctor), or the vaginal lubrication might be inadequate (an application of K-Y jelly will alleviate this problem, or the couple might need to prolong the period of foreplay). Penetration accompanied by pain results in pyschological and emotional damage. The wife may become frightened, fearful of admitting the pain to her husband, secretly angry with her husband, herself or God. On future occasions, she will become tense which will aggravate the problem. The scene is set for angry outbursts unless she confesses the real situation to a caring, compassionate, understanding husband.

Another problem that trouble some women early on in marriage is that they enjoy every stage of foreplay, up to and including penetration, but they never experience that 'good-all-over feeling' we call an orgasm. Again, there are several possible reasons, perhaps she is expecting an explosive climax similar to her husband's, and therefore fails to appreciate the gentler, general sense of well-being characteristic of the female climax. Perhaps genital or manual stimulation of the clitoris has been insufficient (it is now generally accepted that friction of the clitoral area is the key to the female orgasmic experience). In extreme cases, it could be that a thickened hood of skin covers the clitoris preventing the woman from feeling any clitoral sensation, no matter how much stimulation her husband applies. (This skin can be removed by simple surgery.)

Later on in marriage, sexual problems still rear their head but usually for different reasons. After childbirth, it is normal for a wife to feel sore for a while and therefore to resist her husband's sexual advances. Similarly, postpuerpal depression, or the 'marital blues' as it is generally called, can leave a woman lacking in sexual drive. When a husband has waited longingly for the end of the pregnancy so that normal sexual relations can be resumed, and the wife shows no interest, he might resort to the nagging that is born of jealousy, frustration and neglect.

Sexual problems in men

But sexual dysfunction is not simply a female phenomenon. Sometimes it is the husband who lacks libido: he may suffer from premature ejaculation, a distressing condition where sperm is emitted either before or immediately upon penetration, curtailing the act of intercourse. He may fail to maintain an erection, or become temporarily impotent. Men find such problems humiliating. In the absence of his wife's understanding and tenderness a husband's repressed frustration and self-despising will boil over in unexpected ways that will appear to have no connection with sex, but that will disrupt the marriage.

It will be apparent from what I have written that sexual conflict is expressed in subtle ways. How can such conflict be used creatively to contribute to the well-being of the relationship? In an attempt to answer that question I propose to introduce you to John and Claire, a couple who found it embarrassing and costly to admit that, after two years of marriage, the sexual side of their relationship was not only a pressure, but a profound disappointment.

The creative use of conflict: John and Claire

'I feel such a failure, and I must admit I feel a bit cheated by God, too. I mean, all those months when we were going out together we didn't sleep together because we felt that such abstinence was what God demanded. Then when we could have sex we discovered that it wasn't all that fantastic after all. I still haven't had an orgasm. At the beginning I found that penetration was quite painful. Now I'm frightened. I'm afraid John is going to hurt me again, so I feel myself tense up. I suppose that doesn't help really.'

John chipped in. 'I'm disappointed too. I see how miserable Claire's becoming and I keep blaming myself, asking,

"What's wrong with me? Everyone else seems to make their wives happy. What kind of husband am I that I cause *my* wife only misery?" Then I begin worrying. Perhaps I'm too small to satisfy a woman. It's silly. We love each other dearly and we're not the quarrelling types, but I can tell there's a sullen silence driving a wedge between us sometimes, and we both know the root cause: sex.'

No magic formula brought this couple out of the darkness of sexual inexpertise into the light of mutually satisfying sex. But a number of factors helped. These are essential for those who would similarly use conflict creatively.

Talk sexually

The first and most important step they took was to learn to communicate openly about sex: with each other, with God, and eventually in a counselling situation. Like many other couples, neither Claire nor John found this an easy thing to do. Yet, to their surprise, they quickly learned to talk about intercourse as naturally as they chat about the weather. They had always avoided sex-talk before, mistaking such frankness for the smutty story-telling they indulged in during school days. When conflict persuaded them to ask for counselling and subsequently challenged them to learn the difficult task of talking, they discovered how creative such communication can be. It helped each of them to understand the other better, to discover what the other's needs are, to accept full responsibility for their own hurts, 'It's not quite what I thought it was going to be. Sex is a let-down.'

When we express real hurt we can be really helped. Conflict not only taught John and Claire that lesson but others as well. It persuaded them to explore their disappointment together rather than blaming each other. It pushed them into discovering why sex, for them, was divisive, rather than marriage-enhancing. And it persuaded them to search for ways of putting things right so that both partners were sexually fulfilled.

Pray

Conflict over sex convinced John and Claire of the need to pray about their sex life. They had been fearful of doing this earlier; afraid that God would not be interested in this essentially private part of their marriage. With the growing realization that the sex idea was hatched by God; that it was he who equipped the male and female body to fit into each other like a two-piece jigsaw, came the recognition that God also makes a promise to married people: that leaving and cleaving will result in one-fleshness. Out of conflict, beauty emerged, like the setting sun peeping out behind storm clouds turning the whole sky to gold. Out of creative prayer came another transformation: growth in understanding.

Growth in understanding

Claire learned the importance of helping John to understand her sexual likes and dislikes; the value of refusing to expect him to be a mind reader. As she assured him with grunts and phrases like, 'Mm. That's nice', when her husband stroked her thighs or aroused her during foreplay, John's confidence was restored. He knew he was bringing pleasure to his wife and wanted to give her more.

Similarly, John learned to tell Claire what gave him pleasure: the sight of her naked body, the feel of her warm flesh against his, her silhouette glimpsed through a certain nightie. Conflict taught them that silence is unproductive; that it leads to misunderstandings and makes impossible demands: including the demand that the partner should become a clairvoyant.

Confess

Conflict, for John and Claire, was rather like an MOT test. It took their marriage off the road for a while, diagnosed the problem and did some necessary adjusting. The same was true for Ron and Cynthia whom I mentioned earlier in this chapter. Conflict brought them to the point of confession.

One of the causes of Cynthia's frigidity was guilt: the guilt that stained her conscience because she and Ron had slept together before they married. 'It was all so furtive and rushed. And I knew it was wrong. I can never forgive myself and I'm really not sure that God's forgiven me either. After all, it was blatant, deliberate sin. I knew what I was doing but I said "Yes" all along the line.'

Conflict brought Cynthia to the point of repentance, where, with an act of the will, she surrendered all the skeletons in the cupboard to God, luxuriated in his cleansing and forgiveness, and left the past behind. (For a fuller discussion of this, see my book, *Growing into Love*, IVP, 1982, ch.8.)

The creative measures taken by John and Claire and Ron and Cynthia are open to all couples who will avail themselves of them. They are of value because, for most couples, there are times when sexual relations are strained: the latter stages of pregnancy, certain days during the menstrual cycle, illness. At such times, one partner may feel cheated or deprived. When couples talk about these feelings they discover ways of overcoming the frustration: by expressing love through more cuddling than usual, by fondling the breasts and genitals to convey intimacy even though intercourse is not possible, by the wife bringing her husband to a climax by means of manual rather than vaginal stimulation. Wants and needs are made known through the vulnerability of sharing. Such sharing brings couples from scrapping to replanning.

Humour

Conflict taught both couples I have mentioned a vital lesson: to learn to laugh about their sexual mishaps, not to be crushed or humiliated by them. Humour paves the way for progress. Where a couple find that fumbling with a contraceptive sheath spoils the romantic build-up for the wife and pushes her from sexual excitation into sexual irritation, the problem can be laughed at if both recognize the real situation, 'We don't *have* to use this form of contraception.' Similarly, if a couple using the withdrawal method lose interest in sex at the crucial moment out of fear of an unwanted pregnancy, they too can laugh, if they also discuss alternative forms of contraception.

But, of course, couples who love each other will never laugh *at* each other, or use humour to put the other down, or to exploit each other. They will use humour as a route to sex fulfilment and a clear perspective on their problem.

Relax

Conflict highlighted another vital piece of information for John and Claire: to learn to relax as people and to relax about the problem. Overbusyness is a curse. The more couples relax together as people, enjoying each other's company, enjoying God's world together, enjoying spiritual oneness, the more they will enjoy one another's bodies. Challenged by this thought, John and Claire decided to opt out of the senseless round of meetings and activities that consumed an over-large chunk of their time. Instead, they took time off together: held hands again, watched sunsets together, went rambling in the hills on their own. Claire even decided to resign her job, to work part time instead of full time. As they learned to relax, fear and frustration lost their stranglehold. As sexual desire was rekindled, they worked hard at bringing one another to a climax. The experiment worked. To use Claire's words, 'At last I know what you mean by that good-all-over feeling.' The good news about sexual dysfunction in marriage is that it almost always has a resolution if the couple will discover the resolving factor and determine to bring sexual pleasure to the other; if both will relax as people and as lovers.

Abstain

To abstain might sound like the antithesis of creativity. It is not. For Cynthia and Ron it proved to be a positive turning-point.

When couples are eaten up by resentment, fear or anger, and where this backlog of negativity has resulted in frigidity, impotence or open hostility, conflict can become creative when they agree to abstain from sexual intercourse for a prescribed period and for a threefold purpose: to pray, to re-evaluate and to experiment.

In prayer, they agree to hand over the full extent of their frustration to God; to ask him to sift and cleanse it. As they seek to re-evaluate they search for answers to some penetrating questions: Why is sex, for us, such a puny little offering? What are we going to do about it? And they re-read a good sex manual together, such as *Intended for Pleasure* by Ed Wheat and Gaye Wheat. They then agree to experiment with some of the exercises described there without trying to have full intercourse. At the end of the prescribed period, they make love again, bringing to their love-making the wealth of understanding each has gleaned during the fallow time. As Ron confessed, 'It sounded crazy...but for us, it worked.'

Sex within marriage can be the most intoxicating form of togetherness any couple ever experiences. It can also be anguish, hurting and being hurt. The act of total self-giving that is intercourse at its best can unite two people in a deep and luxurious bond of love. It can also give birth to hatred: hating and being hated. Couples who allow conflict to diagnose the problem and who then move on to take the medicine prescribed are those whose experience of sexual intimacy will deepen with the years; those who will refuse to think of sex as a problem but rather will find it a positive source of healing.

12

A Strategy for Strife

To be at variance with one you love is even more harrowing than being out of tune with the russets and browns of autumn. Even so, as we have been at pains to notice throughout this book, the closer people come in relationships, the more they open themselves to conflict. Togetherness invites collision; the two go together. In this book I have tried to explain some of the reasons for this apparent paradox, to show that we need not fear clashes of personality and collision of wills; correctly understood and sensitively handled, the energy they generate can carry us forward into ever-growing, ever-deepening, adventurous relationships.

'Correctly understood, sensitively handled'. This chapter has one aim: to show how to handle conflict by suggesting a workable strategy for strife. The first clue is to know yourself.

Know yourself

Different people react to tension in different ways. And people react to strife in different ways on different occasions. I rediscovered these facts while the outline for this chapter was still taking shape; in fact, while I was leading a discussion group.

For most of the evening, relationships in the group were happy and harmonious. Members of the group were each contributing to the discussion in a helpful, integrative way. As each handed over pieces of the verbal jigsaw a complete picture was emerging.

Out of the blue, it seemed, someone asked a provocative question. This caused a violent reaction from a woman on the opposite side of the room. The smile disappeared from her face and was replaced by thunder-black looks. Her strident voice brought the discussion to an abrupt halt. Other members of the group grew tense. And an ugly, jarring, discordant note was struck in the group. To change the metaphor, it was rather like standing in a bus queue and suddenly being pushed from behind so that each person fell on to the one in front; so that each mistrusted and disliked the other.

We had strayed on to a theological minefield and the varying reactions of the group were fascinating. Some shuffled to the edge of their seats, obviously relishing the idea of a verbal ding-dong. Others edged themselves deeper and deeper into their chairs obviously dreading what was to come. Others looked confused and alarmed.

It so happened that this situation was defused harmlessly. But I reflect later that these reflex actions could have resulted in an ugly group-dissection. For me, this was a timely and solemn reminder that conflict in relationships produces a series of ripples because of the varying reactions conflict sparks off: aggression, defensiveness, criticism, insecurity, mistrust, pretence: the pretence that nothing untoward is happening.

It is important that each of us recognizes how we normally respond to such a situation. One simple way to do this is to ask yourself, 'How might I have reacted if I had been a member of that group?' Another is to read on until you find yourself mirrored in this chapter.

Conflict-enjoying

Some people enjoy conflict. They recognize that conflict need not destroy good relationships but can, in fact, enhance them. Whenever they smell conflict in the air, therefore, they roll up their sleeves and prepare to do battle, not in order to defeat their opponent, but in order to win a victory over the evil that would separate them from the person with whom they are at variance. Many extroverts are conflict-enjoying people.

They differ from the insecure types who enjoy conflict for another reason: the same reason as an aggressive chess player takes on a series of opponents—to win. These people enjoy the challenge of conflict but they lack the generosity of heart that aims for the best, that is, the most healing solution. They fight to win.

Conflict phobia

At the other end of the scale are those who suffer from conflict phobia. Their view of conflict is totally negative. They believe it is always bad, so they avoid it at all costs. They would rather placate their opponent than risk a quarrel. Such pseudo-humility sometimes masquerades for Christlikeness. But Jesus did not model this anything-for-a-quiet life mentality. Where evil needed to be confronted, he confronted it with boldness, even when it existed in his friend, Peter, to whom he was heard to say: 'Get thee behind me Satan.' Conflict-avoidance does not result in peace but in stalemate; in stunted growth.

Conflict-denying

Another set of people have a curious head-in-the-sand capacity. Even when tension is smouldering in a group, community or family they either fail to detect it or they refuse to acknowledge it. They suppress or eliminate tension at all costs. These people often deceive themselves by living with the hope that if they refuse to admit the presence of divisiveness it will melt away, like snow at the end of winter. What is far more likely to happen is that bitterness, resentment and joylessness will creep under the relationship, like beetles crawling under a boulder in the garden, take up residence there, breed and make their presence felt on a series of subsequent occasions.

Conflict-resolving

Others recognize that conflict is to relationships what grit is to an oyster, a seemingly unwelcome intrusion without which priceless beauty cannot take place. These people resolve neither to fear conflict nor to deny it but so to work at it that the result is reconciliation, adventure, peace and growth. In diagrammatic terms, this movement towards reconciliation looks like this:

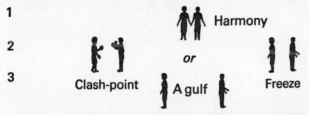

1   Harmony

2   *or*

3   Clash-point   A gulf   Freeze

Here we have two people enjoying a harmonious relationship. Because they are close, conflict erupts, and either heated emotions boil over and they clash, or feelings are so powerful that they are pushed out of sight and the opponents freeze. What happens next is that they take a few steps back from one another. This recoiling results in a divide: a gulf. At this stage of proceedings, the gulf is neutral and necessary. It provides all concerned with the opportunity they need to confront extreme and mixed emotions: anger, hatred, resentment, desire to retaliate, longing for reconciliation, mediation and growth. This phase is crucial to the relationship: the make-or-break point. Conflict-avoiders, conflict-deniers and certain conflict-enjoyers will fail to do this.

Confront

Their refusal to confront the conflict and work through it will result in this:

The gulf widens

The gulf between them is not only perpetuated, it widens. Any remaining relationship will be characterized by competition, bargaining, resentment, ambivalence and pockets of poison that burst open in unexpected and unwelcome ways. In other words, the relationship will deteriorate.

Conflict-resolving people, on the other hand, that is, persons who are determined to lessen the gap, not to broaden it, will both do everything in their power to ensure that this happens:

Reconciliation

Because they have sought to understand one another and the nature of the conflict, because they have each been prepared to tip out the rubble of inappropriate anger, bitterness and smouldering resentment at the foot of the cross, because they have been prepared to apply the healing balm of forgiveness to the relationship, and because they have separately exposed any hurts inflicted to the healing hand of God, they are able to enjoy an even closer, more deeply harmonious relationship than they experienced before the rift took place. What is more, a sense of adventure, fun, even of excitement, steals over the entire relationship, making it richer than it was before.

It will follow from this oversimplified summary of relationship-conflict-procedure that we not only need to know ourselves, we also need the grace of God to let go of the clutter of our negative emotions, and the humility to come to the cross with our opponent and there be reconciled. Certain attitudes are crucial if couples are to work their way through this valley of weeping in such a way that it becomes a place of springs. The first essential ingredient is the ability to confront.

Christlike confrontation

Jesus was unafraid of open, creative confrontation. Christians, similarly, need to learn the art of kind, firm, uncompromising confrontation. When faced with broken relationships, Christians should be prepared to fight, not the persons concerned, but the disease that poisons this part of the body of Christ. In order to do this effectively and sensitively, three needs present themselves: a time, a place and a procedure.

A time

While writing this chapter, the postman delivered a letter from a friend of mine who lives in a Christian community. She describes herself as 'a blot on the landscape'; admits that she is criticizing and hitting out at all the other members of the community. This letter disturbed me because my friend is the fourth member of that household to admit that all is not well. They have decided, therefore, to fix a time when they will deliberately withdraw from the hurly-burly of the busy life they lead, take a careful look at what is causing the breakdown of relationships, express their grievances and work and pray towards reconciliation. When faced with such discord, this is the wisest possible procedure.

This time-setting process is not only vital to the health of Christian communities but to Christian families and marriages also. The reason why conflict frequently results in rifts that widen the gap between persons is that they do not do this. Instead, spontaneous conflict erupts at inappropriate times and in inappropriate contexts. A variation of the following takes place in many homes. The husband comes in from work after an exhausting and draining day. He expects to put his feet up and relax. Within seconds of his arrival, his wife begins to pour out her grievances, to make demands, even to scold: 'Another red bill came through the post this morning. You never pay up on time. And you know how upset this makes me. One of these days, they'll come and plunge us into darkness; disconnect the electricity and the gas. And you just don't care.' Her husband retaliates and a row blows up. This kind of spontaneous conflict resolves nothing. But if this husband and wife will earmark a time when they can each voice certain complaints, then harmony can be restored without too much hearbreak.

Certain do's and don't's need to be observed when fixing such a conflict-confronting time. Don't impose it on the husband within the first hour of arriving home from work, the slump-period when he is least able to cope with family conflict. Don't clock-watch. (Clock-watching is a conversation stopper.) Allow plenty of time. Fix a time that is mutually acceptable to all persons concerned. And make sure that each person knows what the gathering is all about. If one expects a companionable evening and the other expects to voice hurts and disillusionment, the net result will be deeper conflict, not conflict resolution.

A place

This homework of conflict requires a place as free of interruptions, as private and as congenial as possible to all persons concerned. It the telephone can be taken off the hook, so much the better.

A procedure: writing

A time and a place are useless without a procedure. There are two possible procedures: writing and talking.

Although some people baulk at the suggestion until they

have tried it and found that it really does work, I still place writing at the top of my list of means of communication. As I have underlined in two previous books (*Two Into One*, IVP, 1981; *Growing into Love*, IVP, 1982), a blank piece of paper offers several advantages over a person's face: it never looks angry or intimidating, it cannot cry and it will not scowl. Moreover, it waits patiently while you find the right words, it offers all persons concerned an equal opportunity to voice their opinion, and it never argues in self-defence. Phil and Jenny appreciated this form of communication when their relationship fell into disrepair.

When they first asked for help it was difficult to find one strong strand to their relationship. Their marriage seemed to lie on the shore of their lives like a ship's carcase. The only glimmer of hope was that they both wanted the relationship to work: 'We can't even contemplate living apart.'

Several areas of disunity presented themselves: sex, money, prayer, communication. After we had wandered through the maze of problems, I suggested that for the next month, they set aside half an hour each week when they would come together and write to one another about a given topic: How can I help to put our financial affairs in order? How can we make prayer the pivot on which our marriage turns? What do I feel lies at the root of our sexual squabbles? How can we learn to communicate?

This couple had been introduced to this letter-writing procedure at a conference for married couples so they were willing to take up their pens again. Each week, they earmarked half an hour, removed the telephone from the hook and wrote to each other: each wrote a letter to the other for the first ten minutes, they then exchanged letters, read through them several times and discussed the contents before praying about them.

Four weeks later, when I opened the door to this couple, their faces told me that there had been a significant change in the relationship. Their eyes sparkled for one thing, and for another, they held hands. 'We're not through the wood yet,' Phil explained, 'but things *are* better. The writing's great—a life-saver. When we sit there with our pen and paper we know we're there for a purpose: to communicate. And now that we're communicating again, we seem to understand and love each other more.'

Phil and Jenny still have a long way to go before their shipwrecked marriage is navigable again. Nevertheless, progress is being made and this motivates them to work even harder at the remnants of marital love that do remain.

Of course, writing is not always practical, particularly where more than two persons are involved. The persons concerned must then agree to talk: openly, honestly, lovingly. But there are problems attached to this grievance-sharing, as the community I have already referred to found.

Talking

They made an appointment, chose a place, allowed themselves plenty of time, but somehow, instead of relationships becoming disentangled, one person was crushed by the others. This compounding of confusion often happens unless an 'intimate stranger', one who cares but can be emotionally detached, is imported. This person's role is twofold: to reflect back to members of the group from time to time just what seems to be happening, to be a communication-facilitator, ensuring that each person has an opportunity to contribute to the discussion and to pray, albeit silently and unobtrusively. It follows that each person in the group must trust this intimate stranger.

When this community met for a second time in the presence of such a person, a great deal of ambivalence was voiced: bitterness, resentment, envy, anger, hurt. As the trusted friend steered the group through this ventilation procedure, she sought to help each person to understand the others, to put themselves in the other's shoes. The appointment lasted for two tiring hours, but at the end, loving relationships were re-established, forgiveness flowed, the air was cleared. That is not to say all the community problems were solved, or that such spring-cleaning is easy. No. Relationships are more complex than that. It is to say that, like a newly swept chimney, the community was free of the dirt that had clogged. People were reconciled: they were prepared to express love again.

Whenever couples, families, households or communities come together in this purposeful, therapeutic way, one thing is essential: the unity of purpose that strives for healing and reconciliation. Where some members of a group, like passengers sunbathing on an ocean liner, leave all the hard work to a few, this strategy will fail. If this plan is to work, every person present, like the occupants of a sailing dinghy, must consider himself crew: ever-alert, ever-prepared to pour out energy that the boat may stay afloat and make progress. Where this hard work is laced with prayer, conflict becomes the friendly breeze propelling the boat in the right direction.

A personal procedure: the 'seven E's'

A personal procedure that takes the sting out of conflict for me is a process I call the 'seven E's'. The first 'E' is to recall the *event*. What was it that triggered off the clash? It helps me to write it down. Then I ask myself, 'What *emotions* has this stirred up in me?' Again I jot them down on a piece of paper so that they stare me in the face: anger, bitterness, resentment, jealousy...

Next, I *evaluate* the situation with God by asking, 'How appropriate are these emotions within one who is being transformed into the image of God's Son?' Are they loving. Christlike? Do they pass the tests of 1 Corinthians 13:4 (GNB): 'Love is patient and kind; it is not jealous or conceited or proud; love is not ill-mannered or selfish or irritable; love does not keep a record of wrongs; love is not happy with evil, but is happy with the truth. Love never gives up.' Or is my emotional reaction reminiscent of the old nature: jealousy, anger, ambition, divisiveness, envy, immorality, party-faction (see Gal 5:20); bitterness, hateful feelings, shouting, insulting (Eph 4:31)? If my emotions do not pass the test of love, I acknowledge that they are sinful: to be confessed; tipped out at the foot of the cross as so much rubbish.

We noted earlier in this book that where conflict exists in potentially powerful relationships, the evil one, the father of lies, is ever-active. In order to become aware of his subversive role in this specific instance I ask myself 'What is the *evil one* whispering in my ear about this situation and the people involved?' I try to be objective; to bring these whisperings alongside the truth. Again, writing helps, I find. I divide my paper into two columns. On one side I record Satan's subtle suggestions that often come in the form of condemnation or oversensitivity or hurt feelings. In the parallel column I record the facts.

That is not to say that I deny my feelings. No. The next stage is to *express* the whole gamut of my feelings *to God*. Negative feelings need to be ventilated. If we give vent to them in the presence of the person who has offended us, hatred and divisiveness are perpetuated. But if we pour them into the ear of an understanding God, he will sift them, keep what is worth keeping and throw the rest away.

This therapeutic outpouring of emotion might be verbal, it might be written, or it might be non-verbal: the sighs, groans, and tears Paul describes (see Rom 8:26). Tears are a language. They sometimes express frustration, disappointment and pain more accurately than words. But this healthy self-expression in the presence of God is not the same as wallowing in self-pity. The self-pitying person clings to his resentment or bitterness, refusing to hand it over. This is unhealthy. When the emotions are out, we must move away from them. In order to do this, I ask God a question, 'Lord, what do you want me to do in this crisis?' I wait for an answer. This might come through a still, small voice whispering within (which must then be tested until I am sure it is *God's* voice), it might come through a passage of Scripture or it might come through the advice of a friend, pastor or counsellor.

The sting of the situation now extracted, I am free to *expose* the raw material of my life to God, to tell him, if it is true, that I am willing for him to change, not the situation, at this juncture, nor the other persons involved, *but myself*. I then put another question to God: 'Lord, how do you want *me* to change so that I become more like you; so that this relationship may be healed?' Again, I try to wait for God to put his finger on areas of my life that he wants to transform by the power of his indwelling Spirit, to keep before my eyes the cross of Christ, the place of reconciliation, to let Jesus' command, 'Forgive, forgive, forgive...' ring in my ears.

I am becoming increasingly aware that just as a wood-carver sees, not a piece of dead wood, but the beautiful figurine that can be brought to life from that wood, so God sees beyond the personality we project to the world to the Christlike personality he always intended we should become. It is one of the mysteries of the Christian life that conflict can be like a chisel in the hand of a skilful God. He can use it to whittle away the clutter that obscures and mars the image of his indwelling Son: selfish attitudes, prejudices, assumptions, habits, principles, lifestyle, friendships. His task is not to disfigure us, but to beautify us.

This transformation from glory into glory is never accomplished in a hurry. We must therefore *exercise patience* while God effects the necessary changes in us: patience with God, patience with circumstances, patience with others and patience with ourselves. And our patience must be laced with trust: that when conflict has chipped away all that is un-Christlike in us, we shall be beautiful, for we shall be like Jesus (see 2 Cor 3:18).

Hidden meanings

To emphasize, as I have done, that there is an urgent need in all relationships for a time, a place and stocktaking

procedure may sound bizarre to some. Think of it this way.
By setting aside such a space in your diary you are implying
the following:

1. I recognize that conflict and intimacy go together, and
   therefore, from time to time our relationship will be
   conflict-torn.
2. Our relationship matters sufficiently to me to work at it so
   that it deepens with time rather than corrodes with time.
3. Reconciliation of our wills and personalities means more to
   me than that I should win every argument.
4. I want to learn to see the situation from your perspective as
   well as my own, therefore I want to lay aside time to learn to
   understand how you feel.
5. Similarly, I want you to understand me, not so that we fight,
   but so that, before God, we unite.
6. I recognize that conflict can be a friend drawing us closer
   together and a teacher instructing us. I therefore want to
   take time to sit at his feet and learn.

Christians who confront conflict in this creative way need
never fear the incoming tide of tension. Though the waves
rush against their relationship, that relationship cannot be
smashed to pieces. Even the fiercest waves do no more than
wash away unsightly angularities, thus making the relationship smoother.

Five years ago, friends of mine bought a derelict farm-
house which, when I first visited it, seemed little more than
a heap of rubble. That building now houses a community of
forty people who have committed their lives to one another,
to Christ and to a common purpose: to create a loving
community that will nurture each community member,
minister to a needy world and bring glory to God. When
Christians—couples, friends, households, communities
—prayerfully take conflict on board as a diligent adviser,
God continually performs a similar miracle: from the rubble
of wrecked relationships he raises renewed and renewable
love. Can there by any doubt, then, that such conflict is a
friend, albeit in disguise?